SPOON FEED NO MORE

Improving Classroom Performance

SPOON FEED NO MORE

Improving Classroom Performance

Practical Applications for Effective Teaching and Learning

Stephen Chapman, Steve Garnett and Alan Jervis

Crown House Publishing Ltd
www.crownhouse.co.uk
www.crownhousepublishing.com

First published by

Crown House Publishing Ltd
Crown Buildings, Bancyfelin, Carmarthen, Wales, SA33 5ND, UK
www.crownhouse.co.uk

and

Crown House Publishing Company LLC
6 Trowbridge Drive, Suite 5, Bethel, CT 06801, USA
www.crownhousepublishing.com

British Library of Cataloguing-in-Publication Data
A catalogue entry for this book is available
from the British Library.

Print ISBN 978-184590694-8
Mobi ISBN 978-184590738.9
ePub ISBN 978-184590739-6

LCCN 2011925274

Printed and bound in the UK by
Henry Ling Ltd, Dorchester, Dorset

This book is dedicated to teachers all over the world – past, present and future.
The job can be incredibly tough but also amazingly rewarding.
Let's never forget that what we do is a good thing.

Preface

The aim is to inspire, not to perspire.

Stephen Chapman

I think a powerful point is of more use than a PowerPoint-less.

Steve Garnett

Variety is the spice of life; teaching is no different.

Alan Jervis

At its best teaching can be the most rewarding, entertaining and stimulating job there is. There is no sitting around watching the minutes drag by. In fact it is more of a case of, 'How on earth am I going to fit all this material into one term?'

Teaching can also be one of the most difficult and demanding jobs. As for the hours, our time in school may only run from 8 a.m. until 4 p.m., but the time notched up at home doing preparation and marking mean that the working day often does not finish until 11 p.m. and whilst we cannot deny that the holidays are fantastic, they are also well earned. Most teachers are crawling to the finishing line by the end of the school year.

Although there are many positives to working in the teaching profession, there seem to have been some seismic changes in how the profession is run in recent years which have left many teachers feeling stressed, frustrated and bewildered. Teachers are given strict guidelines about what to teach their students and many find themselves lurching from one new initiative to another, drowning in a sea of buzzwords and confused about the goalposts.

Given this often overwhelming and confusing backdrop our aim is to make your life easier by:

1 Providing practical strategies that can be used by most teachers, in most subjects, most of the time.

2 Offering insight into various educational matters to help you with your teaching.

We recognise there is no one way to teach; however, there is such a thing as good practice – which is highlighted in this book. In Part 1 we have chosen to focus on what we believe are the key prinples of effective teaching:

The key principles of effective teaching:

1 Using effective starters and plenaries as well as 'da Vinci moments' (more of that later!).

2 Delivering constant reinforcement as a means of embedding knowledge and providing on-going revision.

3 Introducing variety – the spice of life.

4 'Do first, teach after' whenever possible

5 Encouraging students to create teaching materials themselves.

6 Demonstrating and articulating success by modelling the desired outcomes.

From our combined teaching experience and extensive observations in the classroom, together with providing training courses for over 10,000 teachers to date, we are convinced that teaching based on these principles yields the best results.

A variety of teaching approaches is clearly essential as are different patterns of delivery – we are not suggesting for a minute that teaching Maths is the same as teaching Art. It seems ironic that those who have most frequently bandied around the word 'diversity' are the very people who have introduced formulaic lesson structures and ideas, where every lesson looks the same.

For the last two decades or so the teaching profession seems to have become obsessed with finding out how the brain works and how, as human beings, we learn things. This is understandable but until the code for the way we learn is irrefutably cracked, we are best off using our own experiences as a guide.

The ideas we put forward in this book are based on our own teaching experiences, the reports of others and common sense. Make up your own mind about which of the suggestions will work for you, your students and their learning and, most important of all, provide the best results!

Contents

Preface vii

Part 1   **Key Principles** 1

Key Principle 1   Introducing effective starters and plenaries as well
as 'da Vinci moments' 3

Key Principle 2   Delivering constant reinforcement as a means of
embedding knowledge and providing on-going revision 7

Key Principle 3   Introducing variety – the spice of life 9

Key Principle 4   'Do first, teach after' whenever possible 11

Key Principle 5   Encouraging students to create teaching
materials themselves 12

Key Principle 6   Demonstrating and articulating success by
modelling the desired outcomes 13

Part 2   **At the Chalkface** 17

How to present yourself in the classroom 21

Rules, routines and rituals for establishing effective
learning patterns in your classroom 29

Strategies to make your teaching life easier 32

Marking 35

Making your classroom the one every student wants to be in 42

Using ICT to its maximum 55

Part 3   **Tools of the Trade** 61

Forty-five teaching ideas to dramatically improve learning in your classroom 63

1   Getting to Know You 66
2   Back-to-Back Diagrams 68
3   Cliff-Hanger or Soap Opera Lesson 70
4   Concept Cartoons 72
5   Dingbats 74
6   An Errors List 76
7   Finger Puppets 78
8   Educational Taboo 80
9   Heads and Tails 82
10   Living Graph 86

11	Fuzzy Boards	88
12	Making the Most of a Picture	90
13	Multi-Stranded Mystery	92
14	I Went Shopping and	96
15	Pairs Game	98
16	Title Pages	100
17	Pyramids	102
18	Silent Movies	104
19	Snowballing	106
20	Songs	108
21	Speed Dating	110
22	Triangles	112
23	Word 'Splat'	116
24	Seven Monkeys	118
25	Venn Diagrams	120
26	Using Show-me Boards® in Pairs	122
27	Word Memory Game	124
28	Stand Up/Sit Down	126
29	What's the Question?	128
30	Educational Trump Cards	130
31	Relational Diagrams	132
32	Spot the Odd One Out – With a Difference!	134
33	Option-Based Learning	136
34	Carousel	138
35	Using the Spotlight Tool to Reveal a Picture	142
36	Using Colour to Hide and Reveal	144
37	Mixed Doubles	146
38	Summarising Using Shapes	148
39	Multi-Sensory Worksheets	150
40	Jigsaws	152
41	Probing Questions	154
42	Spiderman	156
43	Maps for Thinking	158
44	Collective Memory	160
45	Alphabet Soup	164

Part 4	**The A to Z of Teaching**	167

An alphabetically wonderful collection of insights and ideas	169

Epilogue	177

Acknowledgements	179

Personal thanks from the authors	179
Stephen Chapman	179
Steve Garnett	181
Alan Jervis	181

Follow-up training	182

Part 1
Key Principles

Key Principle 1 Introducing effective starters and plenaries as well as 'da Vinci moments'

The terms 'starter' and 'plenary' are now very much embedded in most teachers' vocabularies and we consider this to be a good thing. The case for starters and plenaries is made especially convincing when you try this simple memory exercise with colleagues or your students. You need a minimum of twelve participants to do this effectively. You could also do this exercise with a class of thirty and try out all the variations we suggest. You will be amazed at how the graph of results will conform to the patterns described.

How to carry out the exercise

Read out the following twenty words to your students or colleagues:

> curtain   chair   window   iron   paper   pen   carpet   crisps   envelope   ruler
> Leonardo da Vinci   book   kettle   coffee   cake

Then say 'five to go' (we will explain later why this is important) before reading the final five:

> bag   shoe   plug   watch   ring

When you have finished, ask your group to write down as many of the words as they can remember. Make sure they don't sneak a look at their partner's words! After about a minute ask them to stop. Typically most people will have remembered about twelve of the words. Now ask your group to put their hands up if they have any of the following words on their list and to check who else in the group has also put their hand up.

- The words you are asking them to look for are the first and second word from the list (in this case *curtain* and *chair*) – you should have a very high hand count on these.

- Let them know that it is very important that they don't have a sneaky look at anyone else's list as this will distort the results.

- Then ask if they have the word before Leonardo da Vinci (which was *ruler*) which should have a much lower hand count.

- Now ask if they have the word after Leonardo da Vinci (*book* in this case) and again the hand count for this should be low too.

- Ask who has the penultimate word on the list (*watch*) and then the last word from the list (*ring*). The number of hands raised for these should be quite high again (as long as you said out loud 'five to go' before reading the last five words).

Your results should produce graphs that, by and large, look like this.

If you don't include Leonardo da Vinci but do say 'five to go':

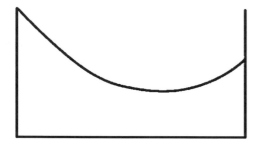

If you didn't say 'five to go' your graph would look like this:

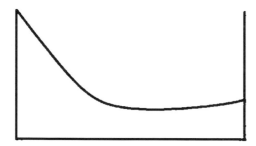

If you do say Leonardo da Vinci and also say 'five to go:

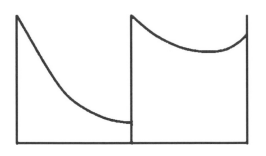

What the results show

The results of this memory exercise are clear. The students' attention is highest at the beginning and at the end of lessons – if they are alerted to the fact that the end is coming. The benefit of starter and plenary activities at these times is evident.

More radically, why don't we have more 'starts' and 'ends' within lessons? For example, if an hour's lesson is split into three twenty-minute episodes, we could have three start phases, three da Vinci moments and three mini plenaries. This would be a powerful lesson where concentration and energy would be very high indeed. The da Vinci moment has the important effect of potentially stopping the mid-lesson dip.

If you have lots of clear starts and ends within lessons you would produce a graph looking something like the one below.

Multiple starts and stops in lessons:

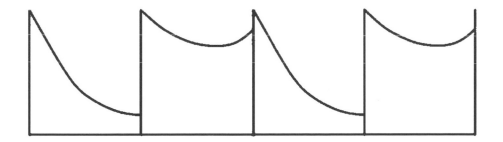

This is known as *chunking* and chunking learning in this way within a lesson allows multiple effects. Another approach could be to divide up the topic focus in a lesson into the three parts A, B and C. Spend twenty minutes of the lesson focused on A, twenty minutes focused on B and twenty minutes on C. Repeat this over three lessons. Teachers tell us that pupils remember far more of all three parts A, B and C than if they simply focused on A, B and C for a whole sixty minute lesson each. We think that the effectiveness comes from mixing up the topics in each lesson rather than spending all hour on one subject. Also the revisiting three times impacts on memory and recall as well as increasing the pace of learning.

Some teachers have noted that when they use the da Vinci moment, the second half of the lesson has been more productive with re-energised and engaged students. It is important, however, to ensure that the lesson content is sufficiently challenging if it is to be delivered within a twenty minute session. There are occasions where it is more appropriate to deliver a section of the curriculum over a longer and more protracted period of time, and in this case splitting the one hour lesson into three parts is not suitable.

Where is the proof that this works?

The *primacy and recency effect* is a phenomenon that has been known for over one hundred years (see Ebbinghaus' Forgetting Curve *c.*1890). TV advertising exploits this phenomenon most effectively and it is an interesting exercise to analyse how an advert is constructed, but also to note that the premium for the first and last advert within a commercial break is considerably higher than for those in the middle.

Further evidence of this technique being used, and therefore supporting the case for structuring lessons in this way, can be gained from analysing the construction of a fifty minute news bulletin, such as *Channel 4 News*. The ordering of items tends to follow this pattern:

1 The headlines

2 An introduction to the news

3 Summary of the main stories/news items

4 The main news items in order of importance

5 A summary of what has happened and a promise of what is going to happen next

6 The lesser news items presented in a progressively shorter format

7 An off-kilter human interest story

8 A summary of all that's happened

9 Goodbyes and a reminder of when the programme is on next.

This structure has been developed as a result of millions of pounds of research into what makes for the most effective programme order to maintain viewer interest. This is why a lesson structure based on the primacy and recency effect *and* the da Vinci moment works so well – and makes for better teaching.

Key Principle 2 Delivering constant reinforcement as a means of embedding knowledge and providing on-going revision

It could be argued that the single most powerful educational strategy is constant reinforcement. The simple premise for this principle is that if you do something once, but not again, you will forget it (whatever 'it' was). This would seem to bear out the adage that you have to do something quite a few times before:

a it really sinks in, and

b you can store it in your long-term memory bank.

Some information or events are so memorable you simply understand and memorise them from the moment you encounter them. Not all learning experiences are like this. If we want students to have a long-term recall of a topic we need to cover it more than once. How often do we lambast Year 11 students at the Christmas mocks for forgetting something they covered in Year 10!

The solution to this problem is to employ a technique many teachers have been using for years – constant reinforcement or 'ongoing revision' as it is now called. It is an easy process. You teach the topic and then cover it again as the starter for the next lesson. You then cover it again in two to four weeks time and you revisit it again after two months, then after another three months and then again before the exam. Constant reinforcement does not have to be introduced at the expense of new material(s) or involve more work. It can simply be the revisiting of existing material(s) but more quickly. The third and subsequent time you visit the topic, it should take a fraction of the time it took the first time.

However, if subsequent visits to the content are achieved through 'new' materials, exposing students to the same content but through a variety of mediums, it will undoubtedly help the reinforcement process. Starters and plenaries give us the opportunity to revisit work too. You could cover work that was done up to two years before in this way. To do this, teachers could start to utilise something we call the 'double starter'.

This does exactly what it says on the tin. The first starter recaps something that was done a long time ago and the second starter recaps something that was done recently. The need for a double starter doesn't really exist in the early part of the Key Stage but as the months go by the need to recap what has gone on before increases, so more lessons could have double starters.

The double starter can also be used to make links across the curriculum and to address key skills and learning strategies used in previous lessons that will be important in furure lessons – both very popular with inspectors!

The other obvious way to recap is to create a da Vinci moment. This is the perfect time to re-introduce a topic the students have covered before with a short snappy activity so as to embed it into their long-term memory.

A lesson structure for the early part of a Key Stage

- Starter (recapping previous few lessons)

- Main body

- Da Vinci moment (recapping lessons from a month or so ago)

- Main body

- Plenary (recapping this lesson)

Later on in the Key Stage this structure would change to:

- Starter (recapping from six months ago)

- Second starter (recapping the last few lessons)

- Main body

- Da Vinci moments (recapping from sixteen months ago)

- Main body

- Plenary (recapping this lesson)

Whilst it may not be possible to incorporate this structure into every lesson, we feel it is worth doing as often as possible. It saves the need for weeks of revision at the end of the course. The starters, da Vinci moments and plenary should be short, sharp, engaging and yield no marking! Who wants to do them if they result in more marking?

Key Principle 3   Introducing variety – the spice of life

There are a wealth of educational theories that a teacher can explore to justify giving their work variety. These range from the visual-auditory-kinaesthetic (VAK) model to the theory of multiple intelligences, from de Bono's Six Thinking Hats to accelerated learning, Cognitive Acceleration through Science Education (CASE), Cognitive Acceleration through Maths Education (CAME), Thinking Skills, Philosophy for Children (P4C) and Assessment for Learning (AfL).

We believe that variety is the key to retaining students' interest. This is because coming at a topic or subject from a range of approaches means that students will be constantly challenged and will develop new skills. Pupils can enjoy a lesson they are really good at one week and the next week be challenged by a format they find more difficult. Students also avoid the tedium of similar methodologies week after week.

We question the notion of 'preferred learning styles' and believe this is flawed. Obviously every student is different – each is as unique as their fingerprints. To take this uniqueness further by suggesting that everyone has their own individual learning style is attractive and easy. The tricky bit is to try to track and label that style accurately.

There are many variables impacting on a student's unique learning profile. It is not simply a matter of trying to work out if they are visual, auditory or kinaesthetic. These three sensory preferences are just one small element of what makes up someone's overall learning profile. A teacher has to factor in other variables such as time of day, heat, psychological profile (are they naturally introverted or extroverted?) and their dominant intelligence. Trying to manage all these variables would simply tie the teacher up in knots.

The following diagram shows all the variables that need to be considered when trying to label a student's preferred learning style. So how do we propose this phenomenon is dealt with? Our answer is simple: do what all teachers know to be a good thing – promote and encourage variety. This way every student's preferred learning style (if indeed they have one) will be used at some point in the term. We have heard it described as 'informed diversity' if you want some jargon!

Individual learning styles

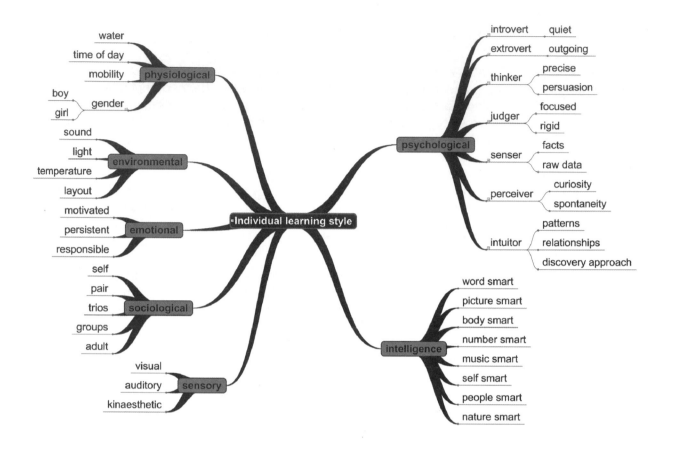

We believe there is a common pitfall that many of us fall into and that is to teach the way we prefer to learn. We are therefore keen to develop a model we call the *theory of opposites.* This is based on classroom practice that we know works well and supports our belief in variety. It also provides the teacher with a useful phrase to capture the essence of variety and creativity that we believe is essential to effective teaching.

If we accept that, in broad strokes, there is the 'arty' side of the curriculum (English, Humanities, Drama, Art, etc.) and the 'techie' side (Science, Maths, ICT, etc.), then what we are suggesting is that some of the approaches used on one side of the curriculum are used on the other.

This can save students from being alienated from whole swathes of topics as happens when a techie subject is taught in a techie style – students with an arty persuasion can become totally switched off. There is a place for a healthy regard for sometimes doing a techie subject in an arty way and an arty subject in a techie way.

We believe that a teacher should provide a wide variety of lessons that develop a range of skills, aptitudes and knowledge that will serve the students throughout their lives.

Key Principle 4 'Do first, teach after' whenever possible

For a long time, many lessons taught in schools seemed follow this format: the teacher would teach something, either via a demonstration, exposition or using a textbook; the students would then answer some questions or complete a task based on the information they had just been taught to check if they understood it. In other words, the teacher 'teaches' and then the students 'do'. If you think about this for a second, the task or activity is simply there as a checking device to see if the students have understood what the teacher was saying.

This is often the slowest way to deliver a lesson. Our suggestion is to do the opposite: get the students involved in an activity at the beginning of the lesson. This activity might be reading, processing, looking, talking or doing. Once the students have processed or even partially processed the new information inherent in the activity it can be reinforced and reviewed.

This process is vital for ensuring that students have a context in which to set whatever it is you want them to learn about. Unless there are specific circumstances that make it impossible (health and safety reasons perhaps), we would always recommend getting the students to engage in an activity straight away for the following reasons:

1 The students are on-task immediately.

2 The teacher is inclined to talk a little less (usually a good thing!).

The teacher should check progress (one way is to use a Show-me Board® – an A4 sized plastic board that individuals write their answers on) and then target what has been missed. The teacher can assess students' individual progress before moving on to the next task. Why spend any more time teaching what the students already know?

The start of a lesson is precious (as discussed in Key Principle 1) so get the students on-task and drip-feed the teaching as and when appropriate.

Key Principle 5   Encouraging students to create teaching materials themselves

We are convinced that there is real merit in encouraging students not only to teach each other but also to create teaching materials for each other. This becomes even more important if you want a bank of materials to support your delivery of starters, da Vinci moments and plenaries.

Getting the students involved in this way builds on the notion of 'do it, do it again and then teach someone else to do it' – an old army method.

Here is the process we advocate using the Venn diagram as an example. First of all the teacher produces a Venn diagram. Next the teacher gets all the students to make the same Venn diagram individually. They then check with each other that they are doing it properly. Then the teacher gets the students to design different Venn diagrams, covering different content but using the same process. Voila! You now have enough Venn diagrams for the year!

The positives

1 Students more readily do homework that is going to be of use to them – and actively used by the teacher – rather than answering a list of questions from a worksheet that will just be 'flicked and ticked'.

2 This is doubly and triply the case when they know it will be marked by their peers and when it is evident that it will help them in their exams.

3 It introduces the concept of students teaching one another – independent learning no less! A win-win situation for all.

The things that could go wrong

1 Some pupils may find making materials tricky – few students could make a decent version of Educational Taboo (see Part 3), for example. The teaching materials they create may be variable! A good tactic to maintain standards is to show examples from the year before and challenge your year group to improve on them.

2 If overdone the novelty of making teaching materials can wear off. Don't overdo it!

Teachers do not have time to create all the teaching materials they would like. Getting the students engaged in designing materials is a simple process with profound implications. If your students are creating games to be used as starters, plenaries or for a da Vinci moment, this will not only save you time but help with their levels of recall. Further examples of resources and templates are included with the acivities in Part 3.

Key Principle 6   Demonstrating and articulating success by modelling the desired outcomes

In order to promote high quality work it is essential that students are absolutely clear what successful work looks and feels like. Make sure they understand what is expected of them *before* they begin a task, rather than tell them what was wrong with it after it has been completed.

So if you want your students to do a perfect press-up, *show* them a perfect press-up. Then, and this part is crucial, make them articulate either verbally or in writing what specifically was happening in that press-up that made it a perfect one.

For example, in describing a successful press-up they may say or write:

- Straight back

- Arms at 90 degrees to the body

- Straight legs

They should not say or write:

- Try hard

- Lots of effort

- Hold your breath

Why? Because these last three things could be present in a poor press-up as well. If we allow them to focus on these last three criteria it wouldn't necessarily yield the perfect press-up that we want. It is vital that teachers keep an archive of work to demonstrate what they do want and also what they don't want.

These same principles apply in any context. When showing an example of a successful English essay, for example, ask the students to articulate in precise terms what are the components of that good essay. Keep making the distinction between specific criteria and non-specific criteria. It might be appropriate to ask for:

- Alliteration

- Metaphor

- A dramatic end

You wouldn't want to ask for:

- Lots of effort

'Lots of effort' by itself does not, of course, distinguish a good essay from a poor essay.

It might seem obvious to suggest showing students what is required to do well. But all three authors were never once shown what it took to get a first class degree at university. We were expected to find out for ourselves! A clear demonstration of an A* piece of work is the best way to clarify for the students what they need to do.

Be specific

Be specific when praising students who achieve the desired outcome. Endless exclamations of 'Well done!', 'Brilliant work!', 'You've tried ever so hard!' or 'Oh bless you!' are not good enough. We have to be specific: 'X was done well because you did Y and Z as well.' Then we can go further: 'You could improve still further by doing A, B and C.' Here, again, you can be specific and demonstrate!

Summary

- A starter activity is vital.

- A plenary activity is vital.

- A da Vinci moment is helpful to avoid the mid-lesson dip.

- Chunking a lesson can provide multiple primary–recency effects but don't allow students to engage with one activity for too long.

- Constant reinforcement improves learning.

- Variety is key to improving skills, motivation and understanding.

- Get students working first and don't always lead with teacher talk.

- Encourage pupils to create their own examples of the activities you show them.

- If you want a successful piece of work, show examples beforehand and ask students why it is successful.

Part 2
At the Chalkface

It's all about you!

This section is all about what you can do to improve yourself as a teacher. It includes:

1 How you present yourself in the classroom:

- Voice
- Body language
- Eyes

2 Rules, routines and rituals for establishing effective learning patterns in your lessons

3 Strategies to make your teaching life easier:

- Using praise

4 Marking:

- Marking strategies
- Rewards

5 Making your classroom the one every student in the school wants to be in:

- Displays
- Music
- Arrangement
- Seating grouping
- Colour
- Smell

6 Using ICT to its maximum:

- Interactive whiteboards
- VLEs
- Film

How to present yourself in the classroom

Voice and body language

There are a whole range of voice and body language patterns that are unique to the teaching profession. 'Don't talk to me as though I'm one of your pupils!' is an often heard plea from the partners or friends of most members of the teaching profession at some point or another.

In this section, we will explain how to adopt what we refer to as adult-to-child voice and body language – voice and body language patterns that are idiosyncratic to the teaching profession. Yes, as teachers we do look and sound different from the general public.

The eyes

Our eyes are a major source of information to others. They reflect the six basic emotions: fear, anger, disgust, surprise, happiness and sadness. In adult-to-adult voice and body language, we seek eye contact with others when we want to communicate with them. Equally, by avoiding eye contact we are sending out a variety of negative messages: 'I am not interested in communicating with you', 'I dislike you', 'I am trying to deceive you', or 'I disapprove'. However, in adult-to-child voice and body language, we often use peripheral vision (e.g. placing students to the side of us) to enhance our adult status.

Here are some ways to use your eyes in the classroom:

- Give the classic teacher stare, which is not to be confused with staring someone out.

- Give a 'knowing look'. We can often get an insight into a person's mood by studying their eyes – this is a chance to read the classroom thermometer.

- Give a reassuring look when students are struggling.

- Praise with a pleased-with-you look (you only need a split second for this).

- Catch a student's eye in the early part of a lesson to let them know that you know they are there.

Females often hold a gaze for longer than males and are more likely to make initial eye contact. For many males eye-to-eye contact can be problematic and some male teachers never make any protracted form of eye contact with any student ever! Extended eye contact is usually only used to indicate either a highly personal confrontation or falling in love/sexual frisson – neither of which we want in the classroom.

A rule of thumb for normal adult behaviour is to maintain indirect eye contact for about two thirds of your exchange with someone else. Any more and people find us threatening; less and they think we are not paying attention to them. We basically want to convey the message, 'I am interested in what you have to say.' We can intensify this feeling by nodding occasionally which transmits further positive messages.

To let a student know we acknowledge they are there and that we value them, we can catch their eye for a second. Our eyes are extremely receptive to the glances of others, and we usually know when someone is watching us and, to a degree, what they are thinking about us. In short, keep your eyes constantly moving around the class. Ideally a teacher needs eyes at the front, sides and back of their head, but given that we only have one set then we must give the impression of seeing more than we actually do. Whilst other aspects of body language are important, none are more so than the eyes.

The voice

It is almost impossible to overstate how important the teacher's voice is: it is our main teaching tool. When students imitate us and our mannerisms, our voice always comes first. Even in today's world of interactive whiteboards, virtual learning environments (VLEs) and computer suites, the main tool for the teacher is their voice. It is no wonder that many teachers suffer from some sort of throat damage at some point in their careers.

Despite this many teachers have had no specific voice training. We believe that, once again, variety is the key. Different voices are needed to teach well.

We have identified six main teaching voices that a teacher should have at their disposal. (There are variations within each type and we have simplified the subtleties for the sake of clarity, but these are the main categories): instruction voice, subject voice, praise voice, telling-off voice, talk-over voice and chivvying voice.

Instruction voice

As teachers we have to tell students what to do. It is vital we work out how to give instructions. Rushed instructions can lead to wasted student time. Our motto would be: Say it once to everyone, rather than to everyone once. Make your instruction voice calm, precise, formal, slower and slightly louder than normal. It should be heavily punctuated with pauses. This is so you can think clearly so that every word is understood. Keep your body still so as not to distract from the instructions and to convey gravitas. Don't use this voice for longer than sixty to ninety seconds otherwise you will sound dull.

Subject voice

Think of this as a storytelling voice. It is designed to elicit interest and enthusiasm by conveying both enthusiasm and content. It demands the greatest variety in intonation, ranging from loud to quiet, from lower to upper register and from fast to slow. It is public speaking! Being interested in your subject will help you apply this voice. (If you aren't interested in your subject, you can't expect your students to be.)

Praise voice

Introduce praise in a lesson as soon as possible. Why? Because it will make you come across as being positive and, as any self-help book will tell you, people who are positive are much more likely to get their way than those who are negative. Introduce student praise early in your lesson and you will reap the benefits. If you delay giving praise until the end of the lesson, the benefits carry into someone else's classroom and not yours! Try to find something to praise early on in the lesson, whether it is the smile on their face or some work from their previous lesson with you.

There are two types of praise voice: one for praising the student and one for praising their work. Make your 'personal praise' voice fast, passionate and higher than when you talk to the whole class. It is the excited voice you need here: 'I'm really pleased with you …' Use it in short bursts only or it will sound trivial. Personal praise is more about *how* you say it rather than *what* you say.

When praising students' work, be specific and use the lower register. This should be much closer to your usual adult-to-adult voice. The 'low voice' indicates gravitas. Make sure the praise is specific to the work, and then try to spread your specific praise around the room by using 'proximity praise'. (Note: Too high for too long will sound insincere. Overuse of 'That's fantastic!' leaves you nowhere to go.) Praise is best offered in short bursts. Like any currency, if there is too much of it, it loses its value. But never be afraid of using praise – it works.

Telling-off voice

There are two telling-off voices: the loud and the quiet. The loud version should be used only occasionally – as little as possible, in fact, but at some point it will be necessary. The loud telling-off voice is like the instruction voice but louder. Heavy punctuation with pauses will prevent squeaking and give your vocal chords a chance to recover. The reason this voice is akin to the instruction-giving voice is simple: when we are telling off we are giving instructions – 'Don't do that, do this.'

The quiet telling-off voice requires the ultimate adult-to-child voice. It is a cold voice, chilling and devoid of emotions. It requires delay (leaving a gap between the first word and the second) and the use of peripheral vision. It is the most powerful telling-off voice. You are telling the student they are 'excluded' from your communication. It is your ultimate weapon.

Talk-over voice

This is a voice designed to be listened to but not reacted to. It should be used to convey information about the topic or the methodology, so it requires a mixture of the instruction-giving voice and the storytelling voice. You use it when you want to impart more knowledge in the lesson, but don't want to stop the class from working. It is a mid-way voice: if it is too dull they won't listen; if it is too interesting they will stop working. Make the voice calm, soothing and clear, with little range in terms of volume or tone. Use this voice in short bursts. Expect only 50–70 per cent of the class to respond to this voice. It is ideal for keeping the pace of the lesson going.

Chivvying voice

This is the world-weary 'we are all in this together' type of voice: non-threatening, non-confrontational and slightly ironic. If you have to chivvy then find it. The chivvying voice is not meant to be sarcastic; it is a voice that acknowledges, 'Yes, it's Friday afternoon, it's the last lesson, on a wet and windy day, but let's keep going, chaps.'

Body language

Positions in a classroom

- Vary your position in the classroom when you give instructions. Consider standing at the back of the classroom instead of the front, especially if the instructions are also written on the board as a reminder. This works well as the students don't know who you are looking at, so are more likely to stay on-task. As a rule, the more able the students, the more you can vary your position when giving instructions. For the less able, stay at the front. This means you can read their body language and discover whether or not they have understood.

- Standing at the front but to one side allows you to use peripheral vision to see the whole class at once without moving your head.

- Always keep your body still when giving instructions; otherwise you can distract the students from listening.

- Teachers rely on arms to communicate much more than the general public. We move our arms and hands to reinforce the point we are making, to demonstrate and to explain. However, overuse of arm and hand movements can be distracting, so be careful.

- Look at the students' faces as often as you can to see if they understand and try to read their body language (otherwise known as reading the classroom thermometer) to check they are alert and engaged.

- Remember there is no more important part of your lesson than the giving of instructions. Get it right straight away and it will save you a considerable amount of time in the ensuing lesson. Link this to rules, routines and rituals!

To start and finish a lesson

- Find a point of contact with the students that enables you to engage them straight away, often referred to as the 'pocket'.

- Reduce all movement of the body unless you want a really dramatic effect (such as in the 'Soap Opera' lesson in Part 3).

- Do not forget to vary the start and finish of a lesson. The 'Soap Opera' offers an effective alternative style of structuring the lesson.

How to convey enthusiasm

For a group, use plenty of movement around the class and general body movement. Try to avoid the 'bruised knee' syndrome caused by bumping into too many chairs. Don't sit behind your desk for the whole lesson or occupy a tiny, three-foot square imaginary island that you never depart from!

- Employ expressive movements (such as opening your arms) and a variety of voices.

- Give lots of smiles and non-verbal rewards such as thumbs up, raised eyebrows or any other ritual you want students to respond to.

- Show surprise – boys in particular like this as it adds kudos. They are still 'cool' but bright as well!

- Enthusiasm is about passion for your subject. If you care about your subject then others are more likely to as well. If you ask students what makes a good teacher, enthusiasm normally comes close to the top of the list.

Keeping an eye on the class

- Stare – the length denotes severity and importance.

- Be totally non-committal – a simple, 'I've noticed' will often suffice. This is a private gesture that says 'Don't do it again'.

- Employ the 'lighthouse' technique – sweep your eyes across the classroom.

- Have eyes in the back of your head. Most of us are not blessed with these but we can all pretend that we are! The secret is not to comment immediately when you spot a minor misdemeanour, but wait until a few seconds later when you are looking in another direction. The students will marvel at your all-seeing ability.

A recap of the essentials of voice and body language

The aspects of voice and body language which affect the quality of interpersonal interactions and over which you can exert control are:

- The pace, volume, tone, duration and diversity of how you speak. An individual teacher's use of their regional dialect is sometimes a source of contention. We firmly believe that teachers should speak as well as possible in class as students need effective role models to improve their speaking skills.

- The use of vocal inflections, expressions and idiosyncrasies of your own, including key words. Train the students to understand your own subject-specific vocabulary.

- Your positioning in the classroom. Be aware of where you speak from.

- Body language: use arms and hands to communicate or demonstrate (we do this a great deal as teachers).

- Mannerisms and expressions. These need to be positive rather than silly; otherwise they will create a distraction.

- Eye contact – never to be underestimated. Make it constant but never maintained with one individual for too long.

All of these aspects of voice and body language are within our control. We may have become habitualised in our mannerisms but we can still change the way we sound and look. All three authors looked and sounded different at the start of their careers compared to how they look and sound now.

Classic behaviour management techniques

Teacher stare

A good teacher stare should always take into account duration and proximity. It should not be held for too long or from a stance that is too close to the student.

Teacher pause

This needs to be used in conjunction with the teacher. It is a classic element of adult-to-child voice and body language.

Delayed response

This means creating reasons to delay responding to a student's endless requests for help in order to avoid being dragged around the classroom (metaphorically of course!). Yes, of course our job is to help the students, but we don't want to be constantly at their beck and call.

Standing in various places in the classroom

As a general rule, stand at the front of the classroom to deliver instructions and content, but then move out of the contact zone once the students start to do the activity. (With more able students, this rule can be broken to good effect.)

Keeping an eye on the whole class and chivvying things along

Comment on someone's actions when you have your back turned to give the impression of having eyes in the back of your head. Strive to maintain the pace of the lesson.

Non-specific praise

Keep to a minimum, but it can help set the tone for the classroom.

Specific praise

Make sure the students know exactly what is required and use the praise to model desired outcomes.

Conclusion

Obviously everyone finds their own style and their own combination of mannerisms when communicating. However, you need to remember that every movement in the classroom is on show. Don't let this inhibit you, but increased awareness will help your classroom control. Teaching is an act! We have thirty people to control, so we would expect to present a different persona in the classroom from the one we take into the outside world. Whilst we all bring our own personality to the job, we also need to do what is effective in classroom management terms, even if doesn't necessarily come naturally.

So:

- Tall, short, loud, quiet, large or small – physical stature and lung capacity do not dictate your effectiveness as a teacher. Some of the best disciplinarians can be physically small yet have a large presence.

- Beware! Those who have natural advantages often end up being the most disadvantaged in the long term, as they get lazy. A highly charismatic teacher may be less likely to use good subject material to engage their students.

- Excellent classroom management skills are not innate; but they can be learnt.

- Even the best classroom management skills will never compensate for a poor lesson.

- The ultimate goal is to find a balance between student expression and teacher control. It is a balance we all strive for!

Rules, routines and rituals for establishing effective learning patterns in your lessons

What happens in the classroom is relatively simple. We train our students to follow certain pathways that are productive and to avoid pathways that aren't productive. We also train them to conform to certain patterns of behaviour. We do this by creating rules they must obey, routines they must follow and we perform rituals from which they benefit. In this way, patterns of behaviour organise the students into positive patterns of work. The rules, routines and rituals make it clear to them what standards we expect.

Having consistent expectations helps to shape consistency of performance by the students, who thrive in environments where there is certainty about the teacher's expectations. Lack of clarity about rules, routines and rituals can lead to classrooms where students are unsettled and unable to develop good learning habits.

The premise we adopt for rules, routines and rituals is that the more challenging the students' behaviour is, the tighter the structure needs to be. The better the students behave, the less rigid the structure needs to be.

Every classroom is unique, so it is illogical to advocate a rigid set of rules, routines and rituals for teachers to follow exactly. Indeed, the same teacher will develop slightly different procedures with two different classes. Here is what we mean by rules, routines and rituals:

- Rules are fundamentally concerned with ensuring the safety of students and other people in the school, and maintaining a productive classroom climate.

- Routines are concerned with establishing patterns of behaviour such as 'coats off; pens, pencils and rulers out; all the class facing the teacher'.

- Rituals are concerned with unique but repetitive aspects of classroom life such as, 'What is the last thing we always do as we leave the class? We all say, "see you next time!"'

The aim of the 3Rs is to establish effective habits in the students. We believe teachers can bend the rules – it is called professional judgement – but the 3Rs work best when applied consistently.

Your classroom should have its own set of rules and you should consider these to be extremely important.

Some things to consider when making your set of rules

- Do you have consistent procedures regarding equipment and clothing and, where appropriate, the necessary health and safety policies? The key here is consistency of expectations and maintaining this at all times.

- Do you encourage a smile from students as they enter your classroom? Should you attempt some kind of personal comment to let them know you recognise them as individuals, such as 'How was practice last night?' or 'How is the play coming along?'

- Do you aim to always set a learning challenge, such as solving today's riddle and putting the answer on a Show-me Board® or in their books? Students then begin to ask, 'What is our puzzle today?' as they anticipate the ritual.

- Do you play appropriate mood-setting music at the start of every lesson – for example, the *Mission Impossible* theme tune or a song related to that lesson?

- Do you have a 'hands-up' policy before students answer questions or do you have a 'no hands-up' classroom? The latter approach puts the emphasis on the teacher to select who they want to answer so that students cannot opt out as they might in a hands-up classroom.

- Do you have a league table of results for your classes? Are they stuck up on the classroom wall in order to build a competitive element (especially important for boys)?

- Do you dedicate a time of the lesson where pupils are not allowed to ask questions? We all know that the second you ask for silence, whilst students are writing for example, someone will break it. However, rather than say something inappropriate and then be told off, they instead ask a question when in fact what they are seeking to do is break the silence.

- Do you have a part of the classroom (e.g. a bookcase or display) that can be a 'challenge zone'? By using this area frequently, students will know that once they have completed the main part of the lesson they can find an ambitious activity or resource here that will challenge their thinking or extend their learning. Instead of more of the same, they can find a genuine extension activity.

- Do pupils recognise that parts of the lessons are dedicated 'quiet time' where little or no talking is allowed? These may be accompanied by music – classical or other soothing alternatives – which helps to drown out white noise such as corridor noise, clanking heating systems or ground and site staff working outside.

- Do you have a clear sanctions policy that pupils understand and which you follow through? Do students know, for example, that sometimes parents are invited in to sit with their son or daughter if their behaviour is inappropriate?

- Do you have a homework policy that students understand and follow? Do you have the homework written up in a distinctive colour in the top right of your whiteboard? (You then don't need to rush to write it up at the end of the lesson.) Do you have homework slips that are stuck in their books during the lesson?

- Do you always have an exit strategy for the end of lessons such as 'one row at a time'? Do you try to make the end of lessons as personal and engaging as the beginning? Do you smile as students leave? Should you thank them when they have worked well? Should relationships be built where you want the pupils 'eating out of your hand' rather than being 'under your thumb'?

Strategies to make your teaching life easier

Praise

Teachers will have heard phrases such as 'five pats for every slap' that advocate a praise/admonish ratio in the classroom. We have heard it said that praise is the single most powerful motivational force known to humankind provided it is genuine and focused. Quite important then! However, there are ways of praising students that are more effective than others. None will do any harm but it is worth reflecting on the types of praise you use and the different approaches to praise you can take.

It is useful to divide ways of praising into categories:

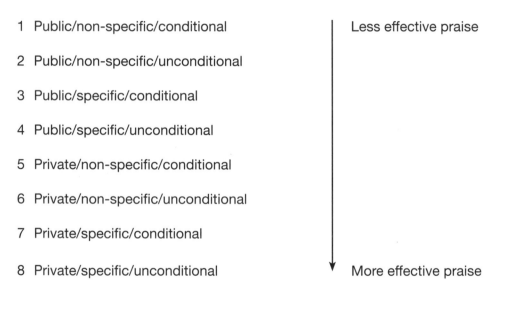

1 Public/non-specific/conditional   Less effective praise

2 Public/non-specific/unconditional

3 Public/specific/conditional

4 Public/specific/unconditional

5 Private/non-specific/conditional

6 Private/non-specific/unconditional

7 Private/specific/conditional

8 Private/specific/unconditional   More effective praise

Here are some examples of each:

1 Public/non-specific/conditional

> 'Well done everyone today – you were great. Please make sure you are like this again next lesson.'

The class feels as if they are being praised but no one knows exactly what they are being praised for. The last comment suggests a sting in the tail. This is the least effective kind of praise.

2 Public/non-specific/unconditional

> 'Well done everyone today – you were great. See you again next lesson!'

The class feel that they are being praised but again no one knows what for. At least at the end there is no sting in the tail.

3 Public/specific/conditional

> 'Well done everyone today – you were great. You lined up quietly like I asked and you all stood silently behind your desks at the beginning. Please make sure you are like this again next lesson.'

Positive effect of the specific praise is undermined by the teacher's last comment.

4 Public/specific/unconditional

> 'Well done everyone today – you were great. You lined up quietly like I asked and you all stood silently behind your desks at the beginning. See you again next lesson!'

Now we will consider the more powerful types of praise that focus on the individual.

(Please note: If asking a student to wait behind at the end of lesson always ensure there is another student or adult around – never be on your own.)

5 Private/non-specific/conditional

> 'David/Diana, you have been really good today. Please make sure you are again next lesson.'

David or Diana knows they are being praised but is not sure why and again there is a sting in the tail. This is the least effective type of private praise.

6 Private/non-specific/unconditional

> 'David/Diana, you have been really good today, thank you! See you next lesson.'

This type of praise is better but the student still doesn't know why they were so good.

7 Private/specific/conditional

> 'David/Diana, you have been really good today: you listened to your partner really well. Please make sure you are like that again next lesson.'

A clearer explanation of why they were good but again there is a sting in the tail.

8 Private/specific/unconditional

> 'David/Diana, you have been really good today: you listened to your partner really well and I liked the way you used the glossary to check the spellings in your work. Thank you! See you next lesson.'

This is the most powerful and productive type of praise. It is particularly good for the student who finds public praise difficult or uncool.

Marking

Marking is an essential part of teaching and learning. Responding to students' work through constructive comment acknowledges achievement, promotes positive attitudes and behaviour and leads to an improvement in standards. Let's be honest – how many students would do the work if they didn't think the teacher was going to look at it?

Teachers need to follow an agreed system and consistent procedures in responding to students' work in order to give clear messages to students, parents and other teachers about individual progress. This is easier said than done. Should we mark for effort, attainment or progress? A teacher's response to students' work is sometimes recorded in books and on display, but much of Key Stage 1 work is practical and most of the responses are verbal. A great deal of praise is given verbally and we use our judgement as professionals in a constructive way when working with young learners to take them forward.

However, the biggest problem of all when it comes to marking is time!

Think about this calculation!

Say you have thirty students in a class for five one hour lessons a day, five days a week. That's 750 student hours of work every week. Let's deduct some non-contact time and reduce this to 700 student hours of work a week.

Even if we spend only two minutes marking each hour of each student's work, we would have a marking load of 1,400 minutes per week. That is over twenty-three hours a week of marking. Even if we take just one minute to mark and record each student's work, this would still be nearly twelve hours – two hours on Monday through to Friday, Saturday off and two hours marking on Sunday. Sound familiar?

We believe that the most effective way of marking students' work is verbally and by adopting a variety of marking systems rather than just one.

Here are some strategies to improve the quality of your marking and, crucially, to reduce the time you spend on it by getting the students actively involved in the process.

Sixteen marking strategies

Icons indicate:

Teacher marking

Student marking

1 The wedding cake

Give students a specific marking criteria and pass samples of their work around the classroom. Ask them to identify answers that fulfil the specific criteria (this is the top layer of the cake). You can also ask them to look at two criteria, using different coloured pens (this is the middle layer of the cake) and then look for all the criteria as they become more able (the bottom layer of the cake).

2 Speed-marking

Up the ante with speed-marking by putting the criteria on the board (i.e. the entire mark scheme) and ask students to circulate their books. Each piece of work must be marked, signed and awarded a grade by another student. A whistle is blown or a 'bleep' given every minute to keep it fast and furious.

3 What? Why? How?

Students again mark one another's work, writing down one sentence stating *what* the problem was with a piece of work, *why* it was a problem and *how* it can be improved. This helps to reinforce the principle of PEE (Point, Explanation, Example).

4 The Chief Examiner's verdict

Give mark schemes to the students and get them to allocate marks to another student's work. Then invite one or two students to come up to the front of the classroom to explain their decisions.

5 Independent marking

 Give mark schemes to students *before* work commences and ask them to self-mark then peer-mark.

6 Five to three to success

 Identify five things done well in a piece of work. Then identify three things not done so well. Point these out with highlighters. Then get students to write down how the three things not done so well could have been improved.

7 One step at a time

 After marking a piece of work, make one specific comment on how each student could improve their work and give an example to illustrate it. When the students tackle their next piece of work, ask them to write that comment at the top of the page. After finishing this work they should highlight where in their work they have followed the advice or recommendations made in the teacher's comment. If there is no evidence of this then they should explain why they have not done so.

8 What's the question?

 Demonstrate an answer. Then ask the students to tell you what the question was.

9 Colour marking

 Here the students work in pairs and use pens of different colours. Here are some variations.

Different colours are used to identify the following criteria in a peer's work:

a Black = a fact or correct piece of information (something 'solid')

b Green = noting how it could be improved

c Red   = a mistake or something that is wrong

d Blue = indicating that something is missing or to add extra information

Different colours are used to identify patterns or themes. For example, in a History essay on the agricultural and industrial revolutions they would use the following key:

a Black = Industry

b Green = Agriculture

c Red   = Politics/social change

d Blue   = Transport

Different colours are used to identify a point, an explanation and an example:

a Black = Point

b Green = Explanation

c Red   = Example

10 Highlighter marking

The student uses three different highlighter pens to annotate their work after the teacher has marked their answer with just a tick or cross. The student goes through their work using the red highlighter for answers that the student did not know, the blue for answers that contained silly mistakes and the orange for wrong answers resulting from misreading the question. Students can thereby gain a visual understanding of the causes of wrong answers and hopefully, over time, eliminate the mistakes highlighted in blue and orange.

11 Peer-group marking

The teacher presents a model answer to each student. Students then swap answers and mark their partner's work against the model answer. Students are more conscientious and strict when marking their partner's work than their teacher would be. The benefit of peer group marking is that students will make a mental note of mistakes made by their partner and will be less likely to repeat the same mistakes themselves.

12 Envelope marking

Students embark on a piece of work. It is made clear that all students start off with the possibility of an A grade. If students encounter problems and ask for help they are given the first envelope. This contains some helpful suggestions. After opening this envelope the highest grade possible becomes a B. If students are still having problems they are given a second envelope with further hints in it. After making use of this the maximum grade they can achieve falls to a C. This is a highly persuasive technique for getting students to try their hardest!

13 Two stars and a wish

This has become one of the most popular marking systems in the UK. The teacher gives one positive comment, one negative comment and a target or 'way forward'. It is a simple and quick technique although it can become too robotic if overused.

14 Past masters

It is essential to demonstrate successful marking – and what better way than with students' own work. Keep past work and let students see it and perform marking exercises on it. Do they agree with the mark given? Select past work from the thousands of examples you will have at your disposal by the end of the summer term!

15 What's the mistake?

Develop an erroneous model and get students to spot the deliberate mistakes. They can be spelling, grammatical or factual mistakes, depending on what you want to teach. Try inserting six mistakes of each type. This is a great way to get students to look at model answers too.

16 Option-based learning

Give students several answers to choose from and ask them which possible answer is best and why. Ask the students to suggest four ways to improve a model answer, which would turn a C grade into an A*.

Tip-top tips

After marking, collate major feedback points and produce a 'hit list' of positive and negative points and go over it with the class. Ask them to write down these points and tick which ones are relevant to them.

Effective marking should help you to:

- Improve learning by bringing to your attention what it is that the students do and don't understand. Marking helps you to decide which areas of the curriculum you need to revisit or recap the following year.

- Encourage, motivate, support and promote positive attitudes by rewarding success and correcting errors.

- Inform your planning. If students are misunderstanding something then that element needs either reteaching or teaching in a different way next year.

- Promote higher standards by demonstrating what represents a good answer or piece of work.

- Correct errors and clear up misunderstandings (an activity for this can be found in the 'Errors List' lesson in Part 3).

- Recognise achievement, presentation and effort.

- Provide constructive feedback. For this you need to ensure that your comments are focused on a specific aspect of a student's work and say how the work could be improved.

- Show students that we value their work. Often a comment with a personal touch can be a clear way of showing that you have looked and value their efforts.

- Allow students to reflect on their past performances and set new targets for themselves with the teacher's help.

Rewards

A popular strategy adopted in most schools to motivate students is the rewards policy. This recognises good work, effort and attitude by the allocation of a reward such as a sticker, star, postcard sent to their home or phone call made to their home. For many students this approach does appear to provide a good motivational impetus and there is a place for it in the classroom. But it should always be seen as a short-term approach. In the longer term, students need to recognise that the real purpose of learning is that it will benefit them. This is the ultimate goal for teachers – a self-motivated learner, driven by intrinsic and not by external reward.

If there is a place for reward in the classroom, what should it be and what kinds of rewards should be given?

The merit

Let's call any reward that is given to the student on a cumulative basis a 'merit'. (We know there are plenty of different names, such as 'credit', but merit seems to be the most common.

Merits are usually added up on a weekly, termly or yearly basis and given either on an individual, group or class basis. Some students receive money or a school-based reward, such as an early dinner pass. Some schools operate a league table in which different groups, classes or houses compete against one another every week in a variety of areas, such as attendance, merits or detentions. This usually works well as students love a league system, and as each week is a new beginning they can put a bad week behind them. The disadvantages are that some classes feel they don't stand a chance given the students in their group, whilst others feel that too much peer pressure is exerted.

With all reward systems it is best to refresh them every so often, otherwise the students can become bored with it. Use one system per year group or Key Stage and then another system in the next age group. A system with a random chance element motivates the less high-achieving students, whilst a cumulative system tends to motivate the consistently good students. We would recommend using both at the same time.

Vouchers

Some sort of cash or voucher system works well but must not be overdone. Rewards of this type run the risk of preventing students from seeing the intrinsic benefit of hard work.

There must be consistency in the allocation of merits. If there isn't, then the currency is devalued. Some teachers give them out for ridiculous reasons. You need a strong head of year to monitor their usage and make adjustments where necessary. If one department is giving away merits such as sweets and another department is giving nothing, then obviously this imbalance needs to be redressed.

Phone call/postcard home

Many students can be motivated by the prospect of their teacher phoning home to let their parents or carers know they have completed their homework or task particularly well. This is often best used as a motivational 'carrot' to inspire a student who you need to turn around quickly. If you choose this method, after the initial phone call you should build on it by:

- Further encouraging the student with verbal praise and encouragement, making sure it is precise and focused.

- Helping them to see how this new-found motivation is going to make them more successful in school. In this way you can move from motivating via reward to intrinsic motivation.

Making your classroom the one every student wants to be in

The classroom is second only to the teacher in having an impact on achievement. Why not make it the room everyone in the school wants to be in? (Be warned, however: make it too appealing and every time the head teacher takes visitors around the school they will end up peering into your classroom!)

Displays

- Create dedicated wall space for student work that is double-mounted and of high quality. Encourage students to take ownership and authority over this space. Create a rota for students to help mount and exhibit work, changing it every four to six weeks.

- Suggest a set of rules that govern the quality of display space, such as colours, double-mounting, ICT-generated titles, balance between the written and the visual. Decide which students' work, which year groups and which topics to display.

- Identify dedicated wall space that is used for work related to curriculum content. This display work should be legible from anywhere in the room and enter into the peripheral vision of all students. It should identify key learning content. Again, change this every six to eight weeks.

- Encourage older students with graphic arts/ICT expertise to support the production of display work.

- If the display space appears old and shabby, invest in paint to create an attractive backdrop. Use bold and bright colours such as blues, greens and reds.

Some considerations when displaying work

We believe that whilst there can be considerable benefits to exhibiting students' work on the walls, it should be thought about carefully and the following points noted:

- Not all students like having their work exhibited. Some are shy, some fear their work will be damaged and some simply prefer privacy. Be sensitive!

- Can the students actually see or read the work? Who is actually benefitting from the display?

- Work displayed on the wall often needs updating and this can lead to a lot of extra work for the teacher.

Don't be too ambitious with the size of your display. We advocate that roughly 50 per cent of displays are made up of students' work, rotated on a regular basis, and the other 50 per cent of permanent work that is based on the core curriculum. This ratio will vary according to the subject. For example, an Art teacher would display a larger percentage of students' work in order to inspire others and demonstrate good practice.

Using large posters with core curriculum content

Each subject has its own specific posters – a map of the political structure of the UK in History, for example, or volcanoes in Geography. Large posters can be used and hence are of considerable value in filling space.

Key words/vocabulary

The key words and terminology relating to every subject can be placed in various locations around the room. These can then be used to reinforce concepts during starters and plenaries as well as the main body of lessons.

Aspirational/motivational quotes

These are quotes (some famous, others made up) designed to improve self-esteem and to encourage students to reflect and strive for personal improvement. Here are some examples we have enjoyed seeing in classrooms:

Smile at least seven times in this lesson.

You are now entering the 'Academy for Learning' – please enjoy!

This lesson is the beginning of the rest of your life – make the most of it!

And here are some famous examples:

The future belongs to those who believe in the beauty of their dreams.

Eleanor Roosevelt

If you can dream it, you can do it.

Walt Disney

Always remember that your own resolution to succeed is more important than anything else.

Abraham Lincoln

Be not afraid of growing slowly, be afraid only of standing still.

Chinese proverb

Educational placemats

Every time the students come into the classroom they take a different placemat. They can swap it as they go to their desks if they find they have picked up one they've had before. Once made, placemats are a super way of teaching without you having to lift a finger – which is why they are often referred to as 'silent teachers'. There are two major types of placemat:

- *The generic placemat for the topic, term or year.* Each of these will cover a different subject matter and can consist of model answers with marking notes, marked student work, labelled diagrams and even pictures torn out of books.

- *AfL placemats.* Traditionally these placemats have some sort of assessment element and consist of mark schemes, key words, suitable linking words, essential photos and so forth on them. When students ask how you spell a word, you can just point to the mat. Placemats are laminated so that you can ask students to tick off the words they have used so far that lesson with a marker and wipe them clean afterwards.

Wall friezes

Make a frieze using A1 or flipchart-sized paper. First, calculate how many sheets you will be able to fit around the room and then divide your curriculum into that number of topics. Ask your students (the top set approaching the end of Year 9 would be ideal) to draw and label the pictures or diagrams you have assigned to them. These large pictures can be fixed to run around the top of the wall where they will be highly visible.

The main function of the frieze is to give the students a past and a future to their learning. It is best if the images follow the order of the curriculum. You can decide whether you want to include different Key Stages as well.

Hanging mobiles from the ceiling

For most teachers this is not an option because either the ceilings are too low, health and safety won't allow it or there is a fear of students pulling them down. However, you do often see mobiles used in MFL departments to great effect, particularly those based on the 'washing-line' concept.

Mobiles are equally effective in other departments too. A fantastic History washing-line could be strung with clothes through the ages, from suits of armour, monks' habits, Tudor ruffs and Victorian gowns right through to a 1920s flapper girl's dress.

AfL corner/corridor

A good example is a GCSE model answer with marking notes (either drawn up by you or from the examiner's report), set out on a large piece of card or paper. The display needs to be placed on a wall by the door or in the corridor outside the classroom so that the students can see it every time they come in and out of the lesson. These should be replaced every one to two weeks.

Music

There are a number of ways in which a teacher can incorporate the benefits of music in the classroom. Here are some examples:

- If you have access to a school intranet system, download some Baroque music (Vivaldi, Bach or Handel are ideal) and play through speakers plugged into a networked PC in the classroom. This becomes a permanent and spontaneous resource that is easily and quickly accessible for both the students and the teacher from anywhere in the school, with multiple access points.

- Consider buying a number of classical music CDs that can be lent to students for working at home.

- Extol the virtues of listening to radio stations that are dedicated to classical music when doing homework or other out-of-school learning.

- Share with students the benefits of listening to classical music. They are more likely to accept it and use it regularly when learning.

Consider the broad use of music in learning not only to help concentration levels and attention but also to signal a break or change in activity or to greet and dismiss students to and from the lesson.

Music to arrive to

- Beethoven's 'Allegro con brio' from *Symphony No. 5 in E minor*

- Prokoviev's 'Montagues and Capulets' from *Romeo and Juliet*

- Handel's 'Hallelujah Chorus' from *The Messiah*

Creating a mood

- Elgar's 'Adagi – Moderato' from *Cello Concerto in E minor*

- Holst's 'Jupiter' from *The Planets*

- Albinoni's *Adagio in G minor*

Music that energises and uplifts

- Rossini's 'William Tell Overture' from *William Tell*

- Vivaldi's *The Four Seasons*

- Elgar's *Pomp and Circumstance Marches*

Music that relaxes

- Debussy's 'Clair de lune' from *Suite bergamasque*

- Mozart's 'Andantino' from *Concerto for Flute, Harp and Orchestra*

- Vaughan Williams' *Fantasia on a Theme by Thomas Tallis*

Background music to hide 'white noise'

- Mike Oldfield's *Tubular Bells*

- Jean Michel Jarre's *Équinoxe*

- Vangelis' 'Love Theme' from the soundtrack to *Blade Runner*

End-of-lesson music to cement learning

- Mozart's 'Andante' from *Piano Concerto No. 21 in C major*

- Bach's 'Air on the G String' from *Orchestral Suite No. 3 in D major*

- Vivaldi's 'Cantabile' from *Flute Concerto No. 3 in D major*

More information about the use of music in the classroom can be found in *The Little Book of Music for the Classroom* by Nina Jackson.

Ways to arrange your classroom

The layout of a room also can affect student behaviour both for better and for worse. Layout also needs changing according to the activity. Here is a simple exercise to highlight the range of possibilities available to you. On a piece of paper draw fifteen tables and thirty chairs and cut them out. Now on a larger piece of paper representing the classroom, arrange these in ten different ways and think about what kinds of activities would suit each layout. Here are some suggestions.

Horseshoe

Set the tables in a horseshoe shape. It may be that you are left with three or four tables; if so, arrange these in the middle of the room. This arrangement has several benefits. All the class can be seen which helps with the management of the students. It creates plenty of space at the front of the classroom, allowing the teacher to set up electronic equipment such as a liquid crystal display (LCD) projector, overhead projector (OHP) or television, and ensuring that all students have a clear view. This space lends itself to the performance of role plays or demonstrations. Finally, the arrangement affords the opportunity to locate all resources and materials for the lesson centrally on a 'resource island'.

Circles

Move all the tables to one side of the room and place the chairs in a circle. This is an excellent layout for participatory and engaging activities, such as 'Chinese whispers'. In this game content is reviewed by passing information around the circle. The game begins with the first person whispering a statement to their neighbour in the circle. They then whisper this statement – together with an additional piece of information – to the next person. This continues around the group with extra information being added each time. This game also works well when the class is divided into several small groups rather than one large one. This means that the number of extra pieces of information each student needs to process is reduced. The person at the end of the circle shares the group's accumulated knowledge with the other groups. Of course errors are made; the group as a whole corrects these errors when all the separate pieces of information are shared.

Fours

Perhaps one of the most effective ways of improving learning for boys and girls is to sit two boys and two girls in tables of four. This set-up works particularly well for group work in problem solving, investigation and 'making' activities. It allows the teacher considerable movement around the class. The teacher will not necessarily be able to see all the students' faces all the time, however, and will need to move around the class constantly. This is particularly important when bringing the class to order, regaining the students' attention or when reviewing learning or checking understanding.

Rows

No doubt the easiest layout to support behaviour management is to arrange the students in rows facing the front. However, this does restrict teacher access and movement around the room. It also limits the capacity to incorporate problem solving, active and enquiry-based learning situations.

Analysing the pros and cons of a layout

All layouts have their strengths and weaknesses. Let's take this one:

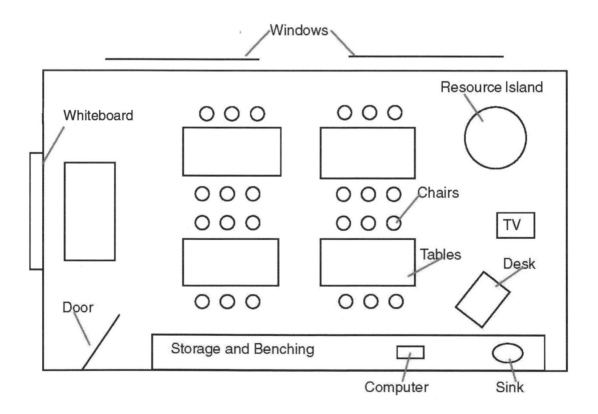

What are the strengths?

- This layout offers flexibility for both the teacher and the students. Not only can everyone move freely around the classroom, but they can also locate resources and change the focus of the lesson at different points.

- Access to the resource island, equipped with all the necessary materials for the lesson, ensures students do not obscure the view of the whiteboard.

- The position of the teacher's desk is deliberately unconventional. The idea is to shift emphasis away from a traditional set-up. Access to the whiteboard for any interactive activities is unrestricted and it allows the front part of the classroom to be a focus for learning rather than a bolt-hole for the teacher.

- Student desks are not located next to the wall. This serves to minimise any opportunities to graffiti or otherwise damage displays.

- Apart from the whiteboard this classroom has no obvious front or back. Indeed, this layout offers the opportunity for learning to be focused on various points of the classroom. A flipchart could be located by the teacher's desk and part of the lesson could focus on material and stimuli on the desk. Similarly this is an excellent location for short extracts of film work. Other parts of the lesson could be focused on the whiteboard at the front. Focusing on displays as learning tools for the lesson is also possible.

- The desks at the front allow students with sight issues to be closer to the whiteboard.

- The desks are broadly concentrated around the middle of the room. This is to restrict the amount of 'glare' which can occur from light reflecting off the whiteboard and affecting students sitting on the far sides of the room.

- Tables of six allow for collaborative, problem solving and investigative learning. They also allow for more creative activities that require space, such as cutting, gluing or sticking.

- Tables of six also free up more floor space for easier movement and access.

- The seating arrangement allows students to shift their focus from one side of the room to the other without having to turn around.

- The area at the opposite end to the whiteboard provides room for demonstrations or mini role plays.

- Groupings of six allows for greater gender integration in seating arrangements. Girls and boys not only learn from one another's strengths but also support one another's weaknesses.

- Groupings of six may also provide greater opportunity to seat students who share similar, or different, learning styles or multiple intelligence profiles.

- It may also offer greater efficiency in the use of supplies. For example the scissors, glue and paint may only be required on some of the tables.

Improved classroom management may also be possible through managing the seating arrangements of individuals who do not work productively together.

Weaknesses

- Tables of six may create too much of a temptation for students to engage in off-task chatter.

- The teacher may feel that classroom management problems are exacerbated with students distracting each other and drawing attention away from the teacher.

Student grouping

Whilst you can't choose the type of students that come through your door, you can choose who sits where. Influencing the position of certain students can have a considerable impact on behaviour. We have all experienced the back row from hell and the front row from heaven, but there is much more to it than that. Here are some suggestions for grouping students:

Boy/girl

The pros of seating students in an alternate boy/girl pattern are that boys benefit from the organisational skills of girls, whilst girls benefit from the risk taking skills of boys. Also girls apparently calm boys down.

The cons are that 'good' girls can get cheesed off when sat next to 'bad' boys and some students get very squeamish about sitting next to the opposite sex. It can also lead to either gender showing off to the other.

Boy/two girls

The pros of this pattern are same as above. The cons are also the same, except that as this is a group situation the negative impacts can be reduced.

More able/less able

The pros of seating one able student next to a less able student throughout the classroom are that able students help the least able, which is of benefit to both the able students who are required to explain information and activities (thus clarifying their own understanding) whilst the least able benefit from constant support. The cons are that the least able don't like to be labelled as such and find it humiliating being helped by a student of their own age. The more able can be slowed down by the least able and feel that their 'reward' for success is to be stuck with a weak work partner. This arrangement can also be wrought with social class and friendship-group issues.

Mixed VAK

The pros of seating students of mixed learning styles together are that it leads to a good group dynamic. Unusual groupings lead to group work that can be very productive with no class or ability issues. It is a type of 'labelling' that the students don't object to. The cons are that there is no evidence that VAK learners exist. There is also no evidence from teachers that this type of grouping has any benefit except for its random selective element which means it is not seen as unfair.

Same VAK

The pros are as above but that learners are similar and so find kindred spirits to work with. Many schools are keen on this type of seating arrangement and argue that it enables students to learn in their 'preferred' learning style. The cons are the same as for mixed VAK.

Same multiple intelligence

The pros and cons are the same as for mixed VAK.

Mixed multiple intelligence

The pros and cons are the same as for mixed VAK.

Naughty/good

The pros are that good students tone down the naughty behaviour within a group context. This suits the classic mixed-ability group. The cons are that the good students get disrupted or possibly dragged down by the naughty students. It is possible that both groups will hate sitting next to each other.

Mixed ability by age or alphabet

The pros are that this is classic mixed-ability teaching. As the criteria are neutral no one is offended and it is seen as fair. Mixed-ability teaching can work really well particularly with younger students. However, many teachers argue that by the time we get to GCSE or A level there is a need to maintain a certain pace in class. Others claim that many A level classes are now mixed ability. The cons are that mixed-ability teaching can lead to the top end being dragged down and slowed down as well as feeling humiliated.

Good at the back/naughty at the front

The pros are that this total reversal of the norm can lead to a reversal of poor behaviour patterns: reward good students for their behaviour by giving them back-row kudos. It means that the badly behaved students are right under the teacher's nose and can actually be helped more. The cons are that there is some evidence that badly behaved students can disrupt a teacher more if they sit at the front.

Constantly changing depending on activity

The pros are because there is no single pattern then there is no constant negative. Students don't get bored of each other and they like variety now and again. Students are used to this arrangement from primary school days. The cons are that it can take a lot of time and effort to organise in class, with some students objecting to being moved and overall class time being affected.

Allow them to sit where they want

The pros are that friends can sit next to each other and do not fuss or whinge about who they sit next to. The cons are that this can encourage a back-row culture with certain friendship groups, resulting in students misbehaving. There can also be too much unproductive talking.

Change every so often (e.g. every fortnight, month or term)

The pros are that this will be seen as fair and no one has to sit next to the student from hell for long. It can promote class unity as students see themselves as 'all in it together'. The cons are that it can be disruptive and many students are creatures of habit and dislike the disruption this change causes. It can also be admin-heavy as the teacher needs to keep an effective record of movement.

Setting

The pros are that students will be in their ability groups for a specific subject. This is particularly good for the top groups. Some teachers claim it is best to teach students like this. The cons are that you might create 'sink sets' where certain pupils are left to rot.

Classroom atmosphere

If you are feeling experimental you could consider how you use colour and smells in the classroom. Most of us do not give much attention to the potential impact of colour in our classrooms. But as any colour therapist will tell you, managing the colour environment can have significant benefits – and not just for the students.

Colour affects us physically, mentally, emotionally and spiritually. Colour therapists believe that the seven colours of the spectrum can balance and enhance the body's energy centres or chakras. They believe that by learning how colour influences us we can effectively use it as an extra boost of energy when the students – and teachers – need it.

The characteristics of colour

Red	Vitality, courage and self-confidence. This is the kind of colour that helps create energy. Motivational posters are best printed in bold red letters.
Orange	Happiness, confidence and resourcefulness. Orange is the best emotional stimulant and strengthens our appetite for life. Greetings and 'smile' posters are best printed in orange.
Yellow	Wisdom, clarity and self-esteem. Yellow is related to the ability to perceive and under stand. Problem solving activities are best printed in yellow.
Green	Balance, love and self-control. Green helps relax the muscles, the nerves and the mind. It helps to create a mood of renewal, peace and harmony. Green is a good colour to use if you have a space dedicated to quiet work and introspection.
Blue	Knowledge, health and decisiveness. Blue is a mentally relaxing colour that has a pacifying effect on the nervous system and aids relaxation. This colour is ideal for worksheets as it helps calm hyperactive children. It is also an excellent choice for the colour of classroom walls.
Indigo	Imagination, dreaming and intuition. Indigo connects with the unconscious self and strengthens intuition, imagination and dreaming activities. Posters that are aspirational and goal-setting are best printed in this colour.
Violet	Beauty, creativity and inspiration. Violet purifies our thoughts and feelings, gives us inspiration and enhances artistic talent and creativity.

The implications of this knowledge for the classroom teacher are that careful thought should be given to the choice of colour on walls, display spaces, worksheets or letters, depending on the effects we wish to produce. Every colour has a potential impact and choosing colours more wisely could help to further enhance our work in the classroom.

The characteristics of smell

Just as colour can have a real impact, teachers should be aware that there are possible benefits to learning from the careful manipulation of smell too. The most pertinent point is that there is a very strong connection between smell and memory. Aroma processing and memory occur in the same location in the brain. Early anatomists called this part of the brain the 'smell brain' as they believed it was primarily olfactory in nature. Smells may trigger a memory either recent or distant. Therefore it is sensible to introduce a distinctive smell whilst perhaps revising a certain topic or key piece of learning. Revisiting the same smell later should trigger recall of that learning.

Certain smells can be helpful in enhancing relaxation. One famous study was carried out on patients having magnetic resonance imaging (MRI) scans at New York's Sloan-Kettering Memorial Hospital. When the vanilla-like aroma of heliotrope was introduced, 63 per cent of patients showed reduced anxiety. In Japan, the Shimizu Construction Company utilises its air conditioning system to release certain aromas in order to improve alertness and concentration, alleviate stress and to relax workers. They also demonstrated how keyboard errors were reduced with the aid of a lemon scent.

The implication for teachers is that fragrances that relax or refresh our students can have a beneficial influence on the overall quality of learning. Some examples of the benefits of certain smells are listed below.

Scents and their effect

Scent	Effect
Lemon, peppermint, lily of the valley, floral scents, jasmine, mint, eucalyptus	To reduce errors and increase work rate
Spiced apple, rose, chamomile	To reduce stress
Vanilla, neroli, lavender	To reduce anxiety
Basil, cinnamon, citrus flowers	To relax
Peppermint, thyme, rosemary	To energise
Woody scents, cedar, cypress	To relieve tiredness

Using ICT to its maximum

There is no doubt about it: information and communication technology (ICT) is here to stay. We advocate a mixed approach to the delivery of high quality lessons that range from paper-based and low-tech to the hi-tech ICT approach.

ICT has the potential to revolutionise learning. The ability to digitalise information has transformed our ability to locate any source of knowledge we like and then store masses of information electronically.

The potential that ICT offers in terms of retrieving information could eventually make the role of teacher as 'information giver' redundant – if you believe some authors! This has massive implications in terms of how we manage learning. The teacher might eventually focus more on individualised support and facilitation rather than whole class teaching. Teaching our students how to 'research, not search' the internet is a valuable skill that is essential if they are to acquire and learn new knowledge efficiently.

ICT also offers wonderful opportunities for teachers to manage resources more efficiently. Everything from the essay typed as a Word document, film clips found through YouTube and Google films, to audio bites of revision topics and scanned-in resources can be digitalised. A teacher's laptop can now be described as his or her 'virtual storeroom'. Properly managed ICT will mean that never again will you bemoan the fact that someone has taken the one and only film from the staff workroom just when you needed it as you will have your own copy on your laptop.

The development of data storage facilities is gathering pace at an amazing rate. The days of the 64MB memory stick are over. It is now possible to have a storage device the size of a small pen in your top pocket with over 40GB of memory. Even this will soon be seen as small. The implications of this for backing up and sharing resources are significant. Both can now be done quickly and efficiently.

ICT can help us transform the experience students have within the classroom. As part of an overall package of variety it is possible to find carefully chosen opportunities to deliver classroom-based content through ICT. In particular, we like the use of activities utilising the interactive whiteboard or LCD projector. These activities should involve challenge and be fun! Exciting Flash designed games together with judicious use of audio and film resources will mean that students don't experience 'Death by PowerPoint' or, to put it more succinctly, 'PowerPoint-less'!

One of the implications behind using ICT in lessons is connected with its ability to offer as much information as is necessary in an instant. This has traditionally been the role of the teacher. The information explosion coming from the internet might start to change the perception of the teacher's role. There has been a growth in online tutorials, VLEs and learning platforms to facilitate learning and there can be little doubt that they are starting to filter into mainstream education. They are the portal to 'house' tutorials and some schools are seeing the benefits of these. They can be used when teachers are absent, they can combine with classes in the library (supervised by a cover supervisor) and the students can log on to material that they can work through independently.

The rapid development of mobile phone technology might mean that in five years time students are actively encouraged to bring their mobile phones into school. This could potentially result in zero capital spend by schools on ICT. The reason for this is that the phones themselves will have all the necessary functionality a teacher requires to deliver ICT (e.g. keyboard and access to the internet).

The implications of this are profound. Learning at its best could be mobile and active. Imagine the Geography field trip where pupils not only look at the feature *in situ* but are then able to write up an assignment there and then, check on the internet for any additional information they need and film what they are seeing too. They then use this information to create their own mini presentations back in the classroom and post it on YouTube. All of this with their phone!

The days of teaching in hot ICT rooms on computers without a mouse, because someone from the previous class has pinched it, might finally be over.

Interactive whiteboards

There are many advantages that an interactive whiteboard (IWB) can bring to your teaching. Some of these benefits may apply equally to using a data-projector with a computer. However, many teachers say that being able to control the software and carry out work at the IWB helps students to visualise and remember concepts, processes and ideas. Some ideas are dependent on the type of software used.

Advantages of the IWB

- Materials and tasks can be pre-prepared and opened on the computer when required. This allows for the preparation of good visual materials. Students have commented many times about the visual quality of an IWB and how colour can help them to understand and improve their enjoyment of a subject.

- Answers can be prepared and hidden in a variety of ways. The task of revealing the answers can be awarded to a student as a 'prize'. This also saves time in writing up answers at the end of an activity.

- Labels can be dragged onto a diagram to label it correctly and items can be grouped, sorted or matched on the board. The only way to achieve this by traditional methods would be card and Blu-Tack or small pieces of acetate on an OHP slide. Using the IWB is clearer and takes less effort to prepare. Just as important – it takes far less time to clear up!

- Being able to turn the page in your whiteboard software means that you never run out of space. It also means that lessons can be structured around a series of pages. This saves having to prepare OHP slides.

- It is possible to return to any page at any time in a lesson, making it easy to refresh students' memories or refer back to previous ideas.

- Links can be created to other resources such as web sites, Word files or music.

- Teachers have told us that they feel their preparation has improved by using a series of slides to set up a lesson.

Virtual learning environment

A VLE, or learning platform as it is sometimes called, constitutes a major part of the government's vision to embrace ICT within education. It is a structure to house a whole range of materials and resources to manage education electronically. This might be school management information, such as student details and data, or it might be resources for the classroom which students and teachers can access. It can also be a forum to improve communication between school and home covering everything from submitting homework to blogging.

Ofsted has said that many schools and colleges in England are reluctant to embrace new technology which enables teaching and learning to continue online and out-of-hours.

In 2009, Christine Gilbert, Her Majesty's Chief Inspector, commenting on the publication of Ofsted's *Virtual Learning Environments: An Evaluation of their Development in a Sample of Educational Settings*, said some schools and colleges were using VLEs as ' "dumping grounds" or storage places for rarely used files, rather than for material that enhanced the face-to-face learning done inside the classroom'.

The report described that in 2005, the government asked Becta, the now defunct agency which promoted learning through technology, to ensure that the majority of schools and colleges made more effective use of technology through online classrooms. They described progress towards this as more of a 'cottage industry than a national technological revolution'.

The report also stated that: 'The best VLEs reviewed allowed learners to reinforce their routine work, or catch up on missed lessons. In those best cases the material offered was fun and helpful … In the least effective examples, documents had been dumped on the system and forgotten.' In some cases the material posted was actually deemed to be unhelpful.

Schools in the UK are world leaders in ICT and have the highest levels of embedded classroom technology in the European Union. With one computer for every three students and broadband in almost every single school, VLEs will soon be commonplace too.

There are a number of different VLEs available, such as Moodle, Fronter, Netmedia, Univservity and Viglen to name but a few. Simply search for the names on the internet and the results will take you to web sites offering sample tutorials and technical information. Many schools are now doubting the validity of a VLE and are looking to the internet as the way forward, not their own intranet.

Film clips

If we wanted to show any sort of film clip when we first started out as new teachers, we had to wheel out an enormous TV and video on a trolley, wind the VHS tape to the correct place, work out the remote controls and then finally press play, with our fingers and toes crossed, hoping and praying the thing would actually work.

Advances in technology mean that things are now very different: you can rip the clip you want from YouTube, embed it into your hard drive or place it on a memory stick, possibly edit it or add dialogue and then play it on an IWB where you could pause it in order to annotate a particular section.

Somewhere in between these polar opposites lies the reality for most members of the teaching profession.

If a picture can say a thousand words then a pertinent film clip can quote Shakespeare. There are so many superb clips that are readily available for free and can make a teacher's life so much easier that it is essential that every teacher knows where to find them.

Sourcing film and video footage

The most commonly used site is of course YouTube. Many teachers have a problem with being able to get onto this site during lesson time and lots of school broadband services are slower than your Wednesday afternoon class putting their hands up, so it is best to rip the clip in the comfort of your own home and place it either on a suitable part of your hard drive or, better still, on an external memory device. An external memory drive is probably the wiser choice as storing film footage can be very memory heavy.

Enhancing your film clips

You can do so much more than simply download and use a clip – you can enhance it so it does exactly what you want it to do. Strategies to enhance film clips include:

- Running additional writing across the screen. These are called 'Astons'.

- Editing in gaps so that students can write notes and not miss anything.

- Adding content by inserting your own sections.

- For the adventurous teacher, there is the possibility of superimposing a person over the top of an existing film clip. This is called blue screen, green screen or chroma keying. So if you want to place a particular student in front of Niagara Falls you now can!

Making your own bespoke film clip

This is surprisingly easy to do. The advantages are that the clip will do exactly what you want it to do. We all have our own way of doing things so a custom-built film clip can be extremely useful. It might seem to involve a lot of work for one short clip, but if you use that clip over and over again it can be well worth the effort.

You have two major options:

- Use a film camera – these are readily available – then edit the film using either Windows Movie Maker, which is free on all PCs, or a more advanced package like Pinnacle Studio.

- The other option is to use a program such as Photo Story 3 and simply insert stills from your camera or clipart and then narrate over the top.

It goes without saying that it should then be your aim to get the pupils to make the film clips themselves, in the same way that they would make a PowerPoint presentation.

Creating a 'classroom for learning' is one of the most important things a teacher can do. This is an aspect of the teacher's work they can have full control over. The impact that a really upbeat and dynamic classroom can have on the students is profound. It communicates to them that you mean business and that you are professional.

Part 3
Tools of the Trade

Forty-five teaching ideas to dramatically improve learning in your classroom

In this section we want to give you some teaching strategies that can be used in most subjects, most of the time.

The diagram below suggests how a lesson could be broken up to accommodate five elements. We do not advocate that every lesson should have the same structure but this is a simple model that can be applied to most lessons.

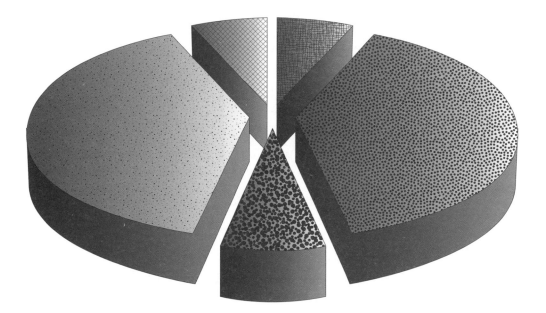

■ Starter ■ Main ■ Da Vinci moment
■ Output ■ Plenary

Adjacent to each lesson idea we have used the following coded icons to indicate where they can fit into your lessons:

 Starter (the first 5–10 minutes of a lesson) This recaps the learning from the last lesson. As the year or Key Stage progresses then it could be argued that there is a lot more re-cap so a double starter can be used (i.e. starter one recaps a lesson from a long time ago and gets the subject back into the students' heads; starter two recaps the previous lesson).

 Main body of lesson (the time where new learning is taking place).

 Da Vinci moment (a point in the lesson where the teacher is looking for a lift in concentration and energy – it could be mid-lesson or a couple of times a lesson at spaced intervals).

 Output (the part of the lesson where we want our students to reveal what they know and understand). This does not have to take place in the lesson – this can be used for homework.

 Plenary. The plenary session is very often linked to the starter of the next lesson so in effect there is a double recap of the main body of learning. If the same activity is repeated as a da Vinci moment, say three months later, then this is a triple recap and really helps place the learning into the long-term memory and understanding. It's obvious that if the same activity was repeated three times this would not be as effective as the same topic being repeated but in three different ways. That's why we need the students to make lots of these materials.

These icons indicate where a particular idea or activity best fits into a lesson. Some activities can be used at more than one point in the lesson and, like many teaching ideas, they are flexible and can be adapted.

Each teaching idea has an icon which indicates the length of time suggested for each activity.

The following icons also indicate which of the key principles from Part 1 are demonstrated within the activity:

 Introducing effective starters and plenaries as well as da Vinci moments.

 Providing constant reinforcement as a means of embedding knowledge and providing on-going revision.

 Introducing variety – the spice of life.

 'Do first, teach after' whenever possible.

 Encouraging students to create teaching materials themselves.

 Demonstrating and articulating success by modelling the desired outcomes.

Getting to Know You

Why it works so well

- This activity provides an engaging way to start a new topic

- It is a good way to discover the depth of prior knowledge of the class

- It promotes classroom interviews

- This activity requires students to talk about the area of study. The activity could be repeated at the end of a topic to show pupils how far they have progressed: each student would have a list of information and walk around the classroom recording student names. A student could then interview these 'experts' and develop questioning skills

What to do

- Decide on a list of ten to twenty facts or ideas that will be studied during the next topic. Transfer the facts onto sheets or boards and give them to any students who don't know anything about the topic

- Students are asked to find members of the class who already know something about their particular fact/idea or any of the other facts on the sheet or board. They do this by going round the class asking other students what they know about this particular topic

- Students who know something about the subject area they've been given present their knowledge to the rest of the class

- Follow this up by asking students to give out the names of students who knew the answer – then ask that (or those) student(s) to provide the answer to the rest of the class as a mini presentation

Summary

- This is an ideal activity to get students talking about their work and for teachers to gauge how much the students already know

- It works well for encouraging students to reveal prior knowledge at the start of a new topic. This knowledge is often far greater than they think

- This is an idea to support the start of a new topic that can also be extended into homework

- It can be used to get the students to create mini presentations and – providing pace is injected by the teacher – it can be extremely effective for kick-starting a new topic

- For differentiation give less able students shorter lists, just requiring facts, and for the more able, provide them with a longer 'shopping list' with more complex ideas. Ask pupils to explain themselves in more detail during these mini presentations, after which they may be subject to cross-examination!

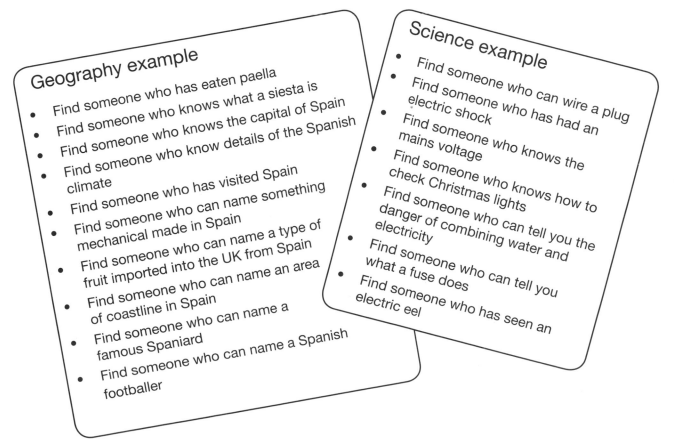

Geography example
- Find someone who has eaten paella
- Find someone who knows what a siesta is
- Find someone who knows the capital of Spain
- Find someone who know details of the Spanish climate
- Find someone who has visited Spain
- Find someone who can name something mechanical made in Spain
- Find someone who can name a type of fruit imported into the UK from Spain
- Find someone who can name an area of coastline in Spain
- Find someone who can name a famous Spaniard
- Find someone who can name a Spanish footballer

Science example
- Find someone who can wire a plug
- Find someone who has had an electric shock
- Find someone who knows the mains voltage
- Find someone who knows how to check Christmas lights
- Find someone who can tell you the danger of combining water and electricity
- Find someone who can tell you what a fuse does
- Find someone who has seen an electric eel

2 Back-to-Back Diagrams

Why it works so well

- This activity requires students to carefully use appropriate language to communicate quite difficult shapes and fine features

- It is a formidable memory task and demands a high degree of concentration

- This activity improves students' ability to divide work into bite size pieces and to turn linguistic instructions into a visual mosaic

What to do

- Identify a key diagram from a textbook – one textbook per pair of students

- Ask students to sit back to back

- One student describes the diagram, the other attempts to draw a version based on what their partner says. This can be done either on a Show-me Board® or ordinary paper

- Swap roles after two minutes and repeat. Students can use whatever descriptive words they like – all they have to do is get the diagram finished!

- Carry on swapping until the diagram and all labelling is complete. When students swap you often hear the 'ah' word as in 'ah – that's what you meant!' – it is a great way for students to learn collaboratively

Summary

- As many students fail to look at or engage properly with diagrams, this extremely effective strategy brings diagrams to life in an active and engaging way that forces them to think deeply

- It is good to use a Show-me Board® and dry-wipe pens when drawing the diagram – it makes corrections easy!

- A good consolidation exercise is to ask students to describe what the diagram is showing in prose

- Feel free to stick the proper diagram into their books afterwards

- This activity has an amazing retention element to it as it simply 'drills' itself into the memory

- The exercise can be followed up by an extensive note taking exercise as well. It is not an end in itself. You would still do all the teaching you normally do but it makes the students interact with the diagram

- For differentiation give less able students a template of the diagram which they then fill in, and give more able students a more complex diagram with additional information

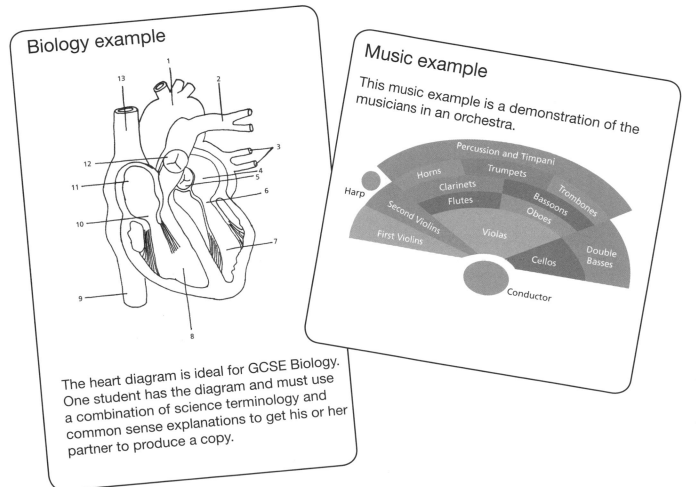

Biology example

The heart diagram is ideal for GCSE Biology. One student has the diagram and must use a combination of science terminology and common sense explanations to get his or her partner to produce a copy.

Music example

This music example is a demonstration of the musicians in an orchestra.

3 Cliff-Hanger or Soap Opera Lesson

Why it works so well

- This is a refreshing return to a bygone era where idiosyncratic teaching can create a 'wow' effect

- What is so effective about this exercise is that it is so different from normal teaching that students won't move from their chairs when the bell rings

- Even students that wouldn't usually stay in their seats at the end of a normal lesson won't leave the room until you've told them what happens next!

What to do

- Select something exciting for the students to see or do at the end of the lesson

- Introduce the idea and really build it up in terms of how exciting it is going to be

- Time it so you know the bell will ring before you have time to complete it

- You play the *EastEnders* theme tune or similar, although this is not absolutely necessary

- Promise to start the next lesson with this activity

- Walk out of the room in a dramatic way

- Do this with your 'best' classes where classroom management is strongest and then once you've got the hang of it you can do it with all classes

Summary

- This strategy is often used at the end of a lesson as a student motivator

- It works on the principle that soaps and novels use cliff-hangers to retain interest for future viewing

- This activity has to be one of your 'wow' moments to really justify the build-up. Aim to introduce this once or twice a term with each class

- Always ensure that the activity you have promised really does happen in the next lesson or else this technique will have the opposite effect to that intended and demotivate students!

- For differentiation adapt the content to suit the less able and make sure the build-up is clear and simple, and for the more able choose a greater variety of moments at which to walk out and have more strands to the story.

Science example

Bring out the Van de Graaff generator in your Year 9 class. Students guess what would happen if they touched it. Students predict what it would feel like if a spark jumps from the dome to their hand. The bell then sounds and the anticipation and excitement for the next lesson is tangible. Next lesson's starter is to demonstrate the generator. This works on the principle that waiting enhances the enjoyment of the promised activity. A teacher who feigns surprise when the bell goes will add to the drama!

History example

The teacher builds up the story of how the events of 1919–1939 led to Britain promising Poland its neutrality and Hitler thinking that Britain and France are bluffing. Develop the story to right before the outbreak of war and then walk out!

4 Concept Cartoons

Why it works so well

- Students look at a topic in depth and need to really understand it in order to transform the information into a different format

- It is a great thinking skills activity in the sense of creating analogies through abstract thinking

- A strong visual element makes memorisation easier

What to do

- Present students with cartoon style drawings which put forward a point of view about a topic in everyday situations

- Have the class make notes on the relevance of the cartoon content

- Hold a group discussion within the class so that students can compare notes and ideas

Summary

- This strategy can be used to make learning ideas explicit and to engage students with alternative viewpoints

- New ways of looking at the situation make it problematic and provide stimuli for developing ideas further

- Not usually funny but designed to provoke discussion

- Multiple 'right' answers are possible

- It forces students to examine material from a completely new angle and makes them think about how they can demonstrate knowledge to others – all of which necessitate higher order thinking skills

- If you accept the received wisdom of the memory experts, it is the transfer of information from one side of the brain to the other that activates high level memory retention

- There are some good web sites for this kind of activity such as www.conceptcartoons.com

- Do a web search for concept cartoons and your subject area

- For differentiation offer less able students simplified ideas and provide more able students with more complicated ideas to process.

Business Studies example

Introduce the students to the concept of a 'growth industry' and ask them to come up with a cartoon to show this. In this cartoon the additional wheels that the caveman has made represent his stock that will be used to supply others.

Science example

5 Dingbats

Why it works so well

- This is a lateral thinking activity that forces students to think and then apply their thinking skills

- The use of visuals and letters makes for an easier whole class activity

- Offers the chance to celebrate the achievements of all students

- Allows left field thinking

- Strong memory element

- Good to focus dingbats on key language/terms

What to do

- Identify a key word or term related to the topic being studied

- Deconstruct the word into syllables

- Think of images related to the sound the syllables generate

- Draw a picture for each syllable and put them together to form a dingbat

Summary

- Great lateral thinking exercise that focuses on key content and can be very helpful as a memory exercise or mnemonic

- If students are able to think laterally there is a benefit in terms of their long-term recall and understanding

- As always it is best to offer an example first so students understand the rules. Some need to be shown a few examples before they get the hang of it

- This activity can create those 'ah!' moments when students realise what word is 'hidden' in the dingbat

- Ideas for the dingbats can come from drawings, images from the internet or fonts such as Webdings or Wingdings

- Not worth doing for too long but great as a da Vinci moment in the middle of the lesson

- The more able seem to really enjoy this

- For differentiation offer the less able a sheet of prepared images. The students can then select the images they recognise or alternatively give them a selection to choose from. Encourage the more able students to use more technical terms

Maths examples

Example **1 3 5 7 9 11 FAVOURITE** Answer: Odds on Favourite

1 **1000000** chance

2 **BAN ANA**

3 **KNEE LAMP TORCH FLASH**

4 **HOROBOD**

5 **WISH ☆**

6 **GOOD**

7 **LEAST** (crossed out)

8 **123 4 5 6 7 8 9 10**

9 **LOST WORD WORD WORD WORD**

10 **ETUNIMANI**

A chance in a million!

Oh!

Why?

1 c h a n c e

6 An Errors List

Why it works so well

- It forces students to spot mistakes that are relevant to their work

- This list can then be used as a preventative list of 'don'ts'

- Students love to spot what the teacher may have done wrong

- Spotting what is wrong is almost better than spotting what is right

What to do

- Simply record all the common mistakes being made by the class over any given period – you may wish to write them in your mark book and build up a list

- Write these common errors on the board or show them in a PowerPoint at the end of that period

- Intermingle this list with some correct sentences or statements

- Students simply have to identify the mistakes in the list – simple but effective!

Summary

- A simple but brilliant way to bring common errors to the attention of the class

- To do this most effectively you need to mark a set of books and make a list of the most common errors the class have made

- It is a superb way of avoiding repeating the same comments or corrections in each student's book

- Don't say it to everyone once, say it once to everyone!

- For GCSE and A level students use the Examiner's Reports from the exam board web sites as the basis for your list

- Always show what should be done as well as what shouldn't in order to make comparisons clear

- Use this with your next year group as a pre-emptive activity. Give the list to the students before the activity and then demonstrate to students all the mistakes that you don't want made

- This is a classic AfL activity in the sense that the criteria for success are made explicit before the students start the work, thus making a better piece of work more likely

- For differentiation include common errors in their list related to simple literacy structure (e.g. paragraph formation for less able students and give the more able longer lists with subtler mistakes)

English example

Ten trivia facts about William Shakespeare:

1. No one knows the actual birthday of Shakespeare!

2. Anne Hathaway was eight years older than Shakespeare and three months pregnant when they got married!

3. Many Shakespeare life facts are unknown – these are referred to as the 'lost years'!

4. Shakespeare's father John was a money lender. He was accused in the Exchequer Court of Usury for lending money at the inflated rate of 20 per cent and 25 per cent interest!

5. William Arden, a relative of Shakespeare's mother Mary Arden, was arrested for plotting against Queen Elizabeth I, imprisoned in the Tower of London and executed!

6. Shakespeare and his company built three Globe Theatres!

7. Shakespeare never published any of his plays!

8. Shakespeare and the Globe actors were implicated in the Essex Rebellion of 1601!

9. Many eminent authors and politicians do not believe that Shakespeare wrote his plays!

10. Some of Shakespeare's family were illiterate!

Answers:
Fact 6 – TWO Globe theatres were built!
Fact 10 – ALL of his family were illiterate!

Science example

Light with a Bunsen hole open?

Use only expensive hairspray when you have a lesson with a Bunsen burner?

Never look directly at a magnesium ribbon burning on a Bunsen flame?

The hottest part of a Bunsen flame is the top of the blue cone?

Never tie your hair back if you are asked to use a Bunsen burner?

7 Finger Puppets

Why it works so well

- Often tricky topics and concepts appear as barriers to learning

- Finger puppets can engage as well as demystify

- Allows for play to find its way back into the classroom

- Works well for older students who want a break from lengthy sessions of note taking

- Can be one of the most memorable lessons of the year

- Good as part of a whole school cross-curricular day

What to do

- Identify pictures of people, animals or objects related to the content being delivered. Cut these out and stick onto card

- Cut two holes towards the bottom of the image – they must be big enough for two fingers to fit through

- These are your finger puppets and can form the basis of everything from descriptions to analysis of key ideas, thoughts, inanimate objects, views of famous people, etc.

Summary

- A fun, creative and engaging way to develop role play. Many teachers and students find role play difficult and are uncomfortable with it. This makes it easier for some!

- A good follow-up homework activity would be to ask students to write a script to demonstrate the activity and to model successful work

- Develop ICT opportunities by recording the presentation. These could make superb films and of course can be used to demonstrate what is required to next year's class

- Shows can be based on inanimate objects such as a hand saw in DT or characters such as Lady Macbeth in English

- For differentiation less able students can be supported by asking them to focus on short descriptions or start off by giving them excerpts of script to read out. The more able can be challenged by focusing on analysis and discussion. Try role playing Mr Lung talking about his relationship with Mrs Heart!

Maths example

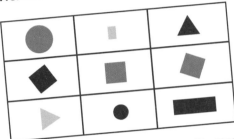

Class working on properties of 2D shapes results in the teacher producing some puppets for Triangles, Squares, Circles and a Rhombus. The teacher uses alliteration to promote some cross-curricular literacy work, with names such as Cyril Circle, Tracey Triangle and Randy Rhombus! Simply cut two finger-size circles in the shapes for student's fingers to fit into and also include smiley faces to add animation! The dialogue is now up to the students.

Science example

Students script a meeting between Albert Einstein and Jeremy Paxman. The question is asked, 'So what happens when objects move really fast?' Einstein replies, 'When objects move really quickly their mass changes and they become heavier.' 'You cannot be serious?' retorts Paxman. 'And even more strange …' continues Einstein, 'time goes backwards!'

8 Educational Taboo

Why it works so well

- This activity develops the skill of providing concise but accurate descriptions of objects, facts or ideas

- It requires students to engage in careful communication and to adapt their explanations according to the responses of the other student(s)

- It forces them to think and speak clearly

- The problem is that materials take a long time to create so why not get your most able students to make them!

- A great value-for-money game that is easily transferable

What to do

- Students are divided into pairs: one of them will be the person describing the word (A) and one will be the person guessing the word (B)

- (A) is given a card with a word or phrase on it. This is the word that (A) must try and get (B) to say/work out

- Underneath the word/phrase are a series of forbidden words that (A) must not use when describing it to (B)

- (A) will give clues to help (B) to guess the word/phrase. Each pair should record the time taken

- (B) has to guess the forbidden word(s)

Summary

- This learning technique involves effective interpersonal communication, creativity and outside-the-box thinking

- It once again forces students to improve their speaking skills and is much harder than it looks

- We do not claim that by using this technique alone we can improve students' speaking skills. However, as teachers we must be aware how important it is that students effectively express themselves verbally and any activity that can help improve these skills is worthwhile

- This activity is very hard but valuable, so persevere

- Make the task more difficult by replacing nouns with concepts

- It only works for topics where the picture demands a shortish response

- Don't use images that could generate a very open and lengthy response (e.g. Lady Macbeth)

- For differentiation the less able can be offered fewer words to guess and also fewer words to avoid when giving clues. The least able can be given prompts to help them spot the mystery word. For those who find it very difficult, you can give out the words that the others are not supposed to use as the words that the less able

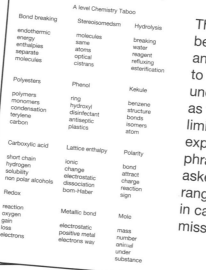

Chemistry example

A level Chemistry Taboo

Bond breaking
endothermic
energy
enthalpies
separate
molecules

Stereoisomedsm
molecules
same
atoms
optical
cistrans

Hydrolysis
breaking
water
reagent
refluxing
esterification

Polyesters
polymers
monomers
condensation
terylene
carbon

Phenol
ring
hydroxyl
disinfectant
antiseptic
plastics

Kekule
benzene
structure
bonds
isomers
atom

Carboxylic acid
short chain
hydrogen
solubility
non polar alcohols

Lattice enthalpy
ionic
change
electrostatic
dissociation
born-Haber

Polarity
bond
attract
charge
reaction
sign

Redox
reaction
oxygen
gain
loss
electrons

Metallic bond
electrostatic
positive metal
electrons way

Mole
mass
number
animal
under
substance

This example can be used at A level and requires pupils to develop a good understanding of ideas as they have only a limited vocabulary to explain their word/phrase. Students are asked to seek out a range of meanings in case their first one misses the mark.

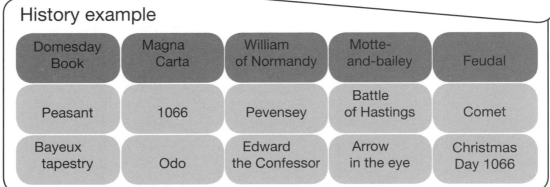

History example

Domesday Book	Magna Carta	William of Normandy	Motte-and-bailey	Feudal
Peasant	1066	Pevensey	Battle of Hastings	Comet
Bayeux tapestry	Odo	Edward the Confessor	Arrow in the eye	Christmas Day 1066

Heads and Tails

Why it works so well

- This activity develops students' skills in note taking and if different students are given different pages it provides an engaging way for them to read around the subject

- This can be a powerful strategy when students are asked to carefully read a passage and create their own set of heads and tails

- Students can use the matched-up heads and tails as a set of notes on the text

- The stand up/sit down variation works very well as it stops cheating and 'Do you get a half mark if he spelt it wrong?' type questions that can plague any school test

- Both are excellent ways to break up a revision session

- At the end of a Key Stage get the students at the front doing the true or false statements themselves

What to do

- Compose at least five statements that are key points relating to the topic being covered in class. The maximum number for a more able student could be fifteen different statements

- Cut each statement in half and either photocopy and laminate them or place all the statements opposite each other on a worksheet that you then photocopy. You can then simply ask students to match up each 'head' statement with the correct 'tail' statement

- A physical version of this is where the students stand and the teacher reads a statement, if the students think it is true they put their hands on their heads, and if they think it is untrue they put their hands on their bottoms. Those who get it wrong then sit down

Summary

- This activity can be used as a paired activity or for students to perform individually

- It requires students to read a text carefully which is something that many students are not good at doing

- The teacher could include an image on either the head or the tail section. Or to make it harder still place an image on both the head and the tail

- As an extension exercise, include some statements that are similar and require careful reading in order to identify the exact match from the incorrect or incomplete match

- For differentiation provide the less able students with statements that are mainly straightforward descriptions of what has just been learnt. Give more able students statements that are a mixture of descriptions, explanations and evaluations

Cubism was a twentieth century avant-garde art movement pioneered by Pablo Picasso and Georges Braque

continued

Heads and Tails -

Art example

1	Cubism was a twentieth century avant-garde art movement	A	painted in oil on a poplar panel by Leonardo da Vinci during the Italian renaissance
2	Andy Warhol was an American artist and a	B	modern and contemporary art museum designed by Canadian-American architect Frank Gehry
3	*Mona Lisa*, also known as 'La Gioconda', is a sixteenth-century portrait	C	pioneered by Pablo Picasso and Georges Braque
4	The Guggenheim Museum in Bilbao is a	D	seizure on 23 December 1888
5	Vincent van Gogh cut off the lobe of his left ear whilst enduring a	E	central figure in the movement known as pop art

Science example

1	An ion is a charged species, an atom or a molecule	A	interaction with another or as a result of its interaction with some form of energy
2	A chemical bond is a concept for	B	to gain understanding of their chemical composition and structure
3	Chemical reaction is a concept related to the transformation of a chemical substance though its	C	understanding how atoms stick together in molecules
4	A chemical reaction may occur naturally or be carried out in a	D	is called its mechanism
5	The sequence of steps in which the reorganisation of chemical bonds may be taking place in the course of a chemical reaction	E	as a consequence of its atomic, molecular or aggregate structure
6	Energy is an attribute of a substance	F	subatomic particles come together to make nuclei
7	Analytical chemistry is the analysis of material samples	G	that has lost or gained one or more electrons
8	Biochemistry is the study of the chemicals	H	laboratory by chemists in specially designed vessels which are often laboratory glassware
9	Nuclear chemistry is the study of how	I	chemical reactions and chemical interactions that take place in living organisms
10	In addition to the specific chemical properties that distinguished different chemical classifications chemical can exist in several phases	J	the most familiar examples of phases are solids, liquids and gases

Match up each 'start' statement with the correct 'end' statement.

10 Living Graph

Why it works so well

- This is a classic example of the theory of opposites where students are using a 'techie' maths structure in an 'arty' subject

- It is recognised as a powerful thinking skills exercise in terms of information processing

- The key thing with graphs is that students have to explain any changes in the graph

- Relatively little writing means students concentrate on the thinking more than the writing

What to do

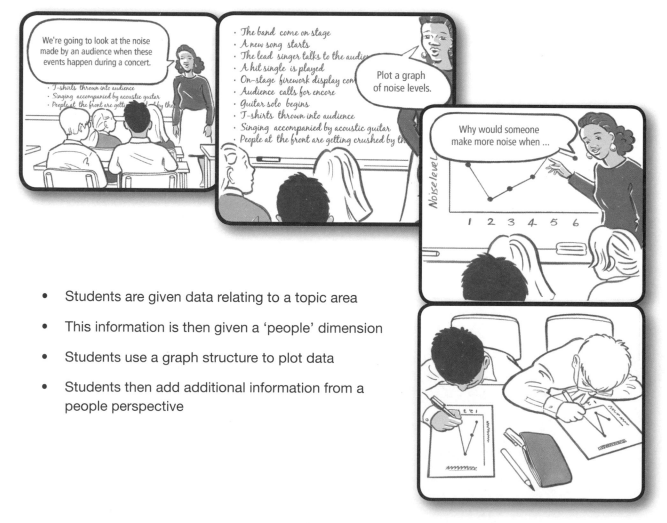

- Students are given data relating to a topic area

- This information is then given a 'people' dimension

- Students use a graph structure to plot data

- Students then add additional information from a people perspective

Summary

- This strategy requires students to be creative when looking at data

- It is also a classic example of approaching material from a new perspective

- It moves arty material into a techie context (as well as the other way round)

- This activity demands that students really consider what graphs mean

- It improves their ability to draw conclusions from graphs

- For differentiation give the less able students simple graphs with less content and encourage the more able students to make sophisticated links between graphs and personal activity

Music example

Examine the noise made by the audience. The students plot how the audience is feeling (on the Y axis using a scale of happy to sad; on the X axis through the duration of the concert) when:

- The band come on stage
- A new song starts
- The lead singer talks to the audience
- A hit single is played
- On-stage firework display commences
- Audience calls for encore
- Guitar solo begins
- T-shirts thrown into audience
- Singing accompanied by acoustic guitar
- People at the front are getting crushed by the crowd

11 Fuzzy Boards

(N.B. A fuzzy board is a backing board of about 100 cm by 50 cm covered in felted material. Words are laminated and Velcro attached to the back. This allows the words to be easily put on and taken off the board. You know the activity has worked when the students are able to recall successfully the whole bullet point from memory.)

Why it works so well

- This can be used as a whole class activity or a paired activity, although it works best in pairs

- Small pieces of card can be used to hide the key words

- The French example (below) is a conversation between two people and works effectively in pairs

- Repetition forces high recall

What to do

- The teacher puts a series of important bullet points on the board

- The class chants these statements

- The teacher removes a number of words from the sentences but the class must continue to chant the complete bullet points by recalling from memory the missing words

- The teacher continues to remove words from the bullet points so that the class have to recall more and more information in order to successfully chant the complete bullet points

Summary

- This is a whole class activity that works as a memory aid for retaining a series of important points

- For differentiation give the less able students fewer words with shorter sentences and give the more able student longer sentences

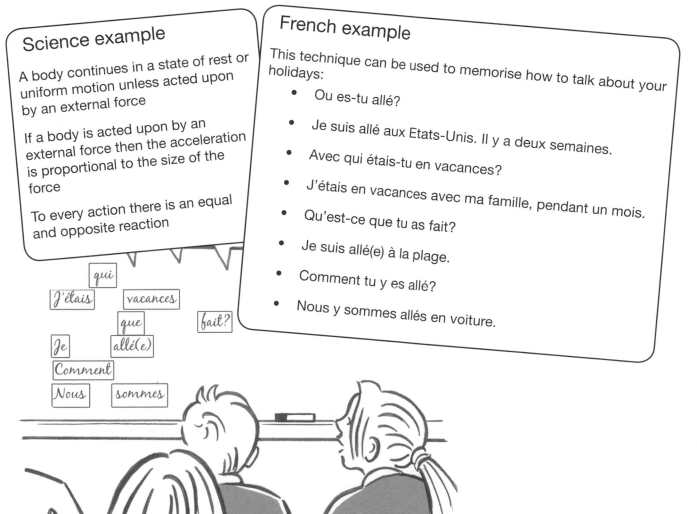

Science example

A body continues in a state of rest or uniform motion unless acted upon by an external force

If a body is acted upon by an external force then the acceleration is proportional to the size of the force

To every action there is an equal and opposite reaction

French example

This technique can be used to memorise how to talk about your holidays:

- Ou es-tu allé?

- Je suis allé aux Etats-Unis. Il y a deux semaines.

- Avec qui étais-tu en vacances?

- J'étais en vacances avec ma famille, pendant un mois.

- Qu'est-ce que tu as fait?

- Je suis allé(e) à la plage.

- Comment tu y es allé?

- Nous y sommes allés en voiture.

12 Making the Most of a Picture

Why it works so well

- This activity helps to promote the examining of a complex situation and breaking it down into smaller chunks

- It demands careful examination of a visual source and the synthesis of individual elements to build up a complete picture

- This is also the perfect opportunity to use an IWB. The simple use of a spotlight tool or screen shade tool or an arrow pointing like a Monty Python hand can get the students to focus on just one part of the picture if required

- You can then go on to the main body of the lesson so much quicker

- This activity takes a few minutes to create but can save you lots of time in class

What to do

- Show the students an image together with a list of numbered features in the picture

- Ask the students to match the list to the image

- Occasionally stop the class to explain any obscure elements if there are any. This is a classic case of teaching as you go along

- Set the task to a timer – the first group to spot everything on the list wins a prize!

Summary

- Many teachers ask students to study a picture or diagram carefully with a view to using it to provide a context to the lesson. However, their observations are often cursory and students can sometimes be unsure exactly what they are looking for

- With this simple but effective strategy students examine visual stimuli carefully. Beware, it can become addictive!

- At the end of the activity the students will have examined the visual image in some detail, so you can build on this by adding additional nuggets of contextual detail

- Ask them to do some follow-up writing on the image, such as explaining where it comes from, its value or trustworthiness. This exercise is not an end in itself but rather a way of drawing much more out of a picture

- For differentiation encourage the less able students to focus on one section of the image at a time and ask more able students to add to the list by generating more labels

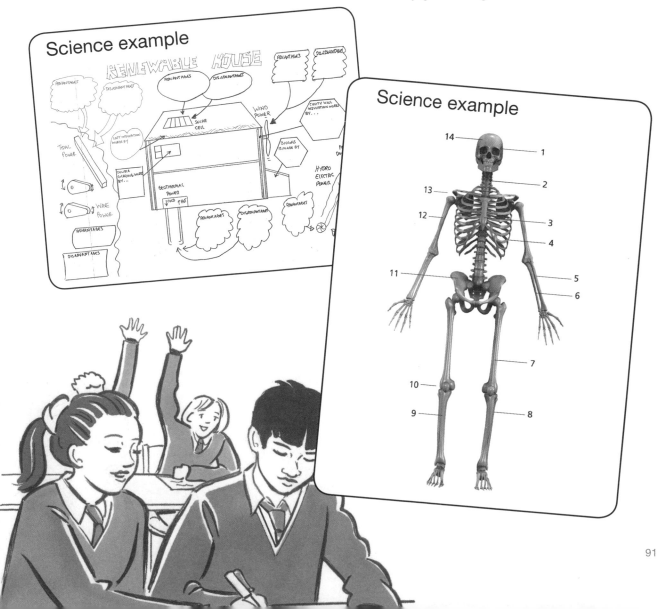

13 **Multi-Stranded Mystery**

Why it works so well

- Nearly all of us love a good mystery

- Most human beings are problem solvers and it makes welcome change to get away from 'chunking'

- This is the type of lesson activity where we wouldn't advocate a da Vinci moment in the middle or even a starter activity. Just get on with the main body of the lesson

- This is a great thinking activity as it requires information processing skills and reasoning skills as well as evaluative skills

What to do

- Students are engaged with a problem and presented with a range of different pieces of evidence

- Students can work independently or in pairs

- The mystery can involve role play, written evidence, photographic evidence and graphical evidence. It is even better if the teacher can pretend to be a witness or if film clips are played to create a context

- The current popularity of programmes such as *CSI* makes this an exciting approach for your class

Today, we're going to solve a mystery.

continued

Multi-Stranded Mystery - <small>continued</small>

Summary

- This strategy requires students to solve a complex problem and follow a range of clues. Instead of breaking down the information into manageable chunks, you will be presenting the information as a whole mystery to solve

- It is very popular and enables the students to really get their teeth into something

- This is an ideal opportunity to develop cross-curricular links and extend the mystery across a series of lessons

- It suits a variety of groups and learning styles

- Have presentations at the end by each group and reveal the solution at the very end

- For differentiation give less able students fewer evidence strands and no 'red herrings'. More able students should be presented with red herrings to challenge them. Also give them plenty of different types of evidence (e.g. film, teacher role play, text, pictures) and more complex issues to decipher

In pairs, for each complaint, answer these three questions:

a) Describe the type of bacteria that caused the food poisoning
b) The source of the bacteria
c) The outcome of the food poisoning

Food Technology example

You have finally made it. Today is your first day as an Environmental Health Officer. Now is the time to make a difference. Today you have received three telephone calls of complaint.

Julie's complaint

Well, it was about 7 p.m. It started with a headache and then stomach pains. At about 8 p.m. I was sick several times and had a fever. What did I eat? Well, for breakfast I had toast and coffee with cream. Lunch was ham and pease pudding, sandwiches and a coke. At 6 p.m. I had takeaway chicken with bamboo and water chestnuts from the local Chinese takeaway.

Peter's complaint

I'm 72 years old and started to feel ill three days ago with flu-like symptoms. I then developed pneumonia. I live on my own and enjoy cook–chill Indian and Chinese food from a local supermarket. I never cook my own food but have toast with jam for breakfast and cheese and pickle sandwiches for lunch.

Carol's complaint

It started at 8 p.m. I had problems with breathing and swallowing my food. I then got a severe headache and was sick. The double vision started to really worry me and I lost feeling in my arm. Last night I had fish and chips. For breakfast I had tinned tomatoes on toast and chicken sandwiches for lunch. I had fish and chips again for tea.

For each complaint:

1. Describe the type of bacteria that caused the food poisoning

2. The source of the bacteria

3. The outcome of the food poisoning

History example

- Why did Geoffrey Goodfellow give up his wealth, his family and his friends to become a monk?
- Why did two brothers line up on different sides in the English Civil War?
- Why was the funeral of Oliver Cromwell in 1658 a 'joyful occasion'?
- Who was to blame for the deaths and injuries at St Peter's Field in Manchester in 1819?

14 I Went Shopping and ...

Why it works so well

- This activity forces students to examine information properly and in detail

- The rest of the class act as judges so it gets everyone involved

- This activity allows the teacher to spot any gaps in the learning

- This is an evaluative activity for the teacher who can make any adjustments necessary to plug gaps

What to do

- Invite five to ten pupils to the front of the class and offer the first pupil an object such as a mobile phone (your own obviously!)

- The first student says 'this is a mobile phone' and passes it on to the next student

- The next student says 'this is a mobile phone and it is grey'

- The next student says 'this is a mobile phone, it is grey and has a brown case' and so on. If a student gets it wrong they have to sit down. The rest of the class have to check that the remaining students have got it right

Summary

- This activity provides a brilliant device to get students to look at an object and then describe it properly

- It is important for students in 'arty' as well as 'techie' subjects

- The activity also encourages students to listen closely and then remember what is being said as well as having to look at an object in real detail

- This activity is particularly suited to moving from concrete examples to more abstract ideas

- Make this a competition by offering a prize for the fullest description given by the last person standing

- For differentiation help the less able students to start the sentence and provide visual clues. Encourage the more able students to describe abstract concepts as well as real objects. Don't allow any errors

Science example

- 1st student: 'This is a mobile phone'
- 2nd student: 'This is a mobile phone powered by electrical energy'
- 3rd student: 'This is a mobile phone powered by electrical energy and uses microwaves'
- 4th student: 'This is a mobile phone powered by electrical energy and uses microwaves that may have a health risk to the user'

And so on until the 5th student says: 'This is a mobile phone powered by electrical energy and uses microwaves that may have a health risk to the user. To send signals around the curvature of the earth satellites are used which are in geostationary orbit.'

Geography example

- A push factor is
- A push factor is a reason for leaving an area
- A push factor is a reason for leaving an area such as a war
- A push factor is a reason for leaving an area such as a war. A pull factor is a reason for
- A push factor is a reason for leaving an area such as a war. A pull factor is a reason for going to an area
- A push factor is a reason for leaving an area such as a war. A pull factor is a reason for going to an area such as sunshine

This is a mobile phone.

97

15 Pairs Game

Why it works so well

- The activity ensures pupils go beyond simple recapping of new knowledge

- Students are forced to make connections between separate words or ideas

- The activity allows for extending the range and depth of students' understanding

- The activity brings about an increase in the number of connections to deepen overall understanding

What to do

Match up each diagram with the correct text.

- Design ten cards with images and ten cards with titles to describe the images

- Put them together to create twenty card packs or enough for one pack per pair of students

- Students must match up the words with the related images

- An answer sheet allows students to match the pairs and to self-mark

Summary

- This is a fun reinforcement activity that allows students to demonstrate understanding and has a strong memory enhancing element

- Make it competitive by rewarding those students who get the highest number of correct matches

- Use a ten by two grid sheet to lay the cards on

- This is a perfect example of an activity that students can make themselves for homework and then bring in to class

- This is also done very easily on an interactive whiteboard

- For differentiation offer less able students fewer cards with less complex words, and encourage more able students to utilise concepts and abstract ideas as a basis for their pairs rather than simple content. Then ask them to add more cards to the pack using their own words and images

Geography example

Community	All species found in an ecosystem
Detritivores	Decomposers
Herbivores	Plant eaters
Heterotrophs (consumers)	Feed on other organisms
Illuviation	Material deposited in lower soil horizons
Leaching	Material that is soluble moved downwards through the soil by solution
Lessivage	Removal of fine clay particles from the soil
Net primary productivity (NPP)	Energy made available by plants for animals
Plagio climax	Plant community unable to reach climatic climax due to human influence
Podsolisation	Intensive leaching

Maths example

Parallelogram, trapezium, pentagon, octagon, heptagon, hexagon, kite, right-angled triangle, isosceles triangle, scalene triangle, equilateral triangle

Match up each diagram with the correct text.

16 Title Pages

Why it works so well

- This activity is creative and allows students to be individual

- It allows students to research the whole topic

- The letters act as powerful memory aids – effectively becoming letter mnemonics

- There feels like there is very little work

- This is a great for a wet Thursday afternoon

What to do

- Students are asked to come up with a key word that reflects the topic that has just been completed. Alternatively offer them the topic title yourself

- Students then represent each letter of the title with a key image from the topic. They are not allowed to repeat images even if the letter is used more than once

- It is less daunting for students if the teacher can give one or two illustrations, so it is vital to model successful examples at the outset

- Students explain why they have chosen the images for each letter

- Insist that each letter has a different image and that they use no more than three letters from a particular area within the topic

- Provide a bank of images from which they can draw on for ideas. Old textbooks are wonderful and students can rummage through them to their heart's content

Summary

- This is a fantastic 'big picture' exercise. It allows students to look in depth at a topic before they have started it

- Picture titles could also be used at the end of a topic. Allow the students to search through textbooks for ideas

- This is also a really good way to sum up a topic

- It can form the basis for wall displays, especially if each letter or image is A4 size

- As always, model an example with your students first

- The pages can become highly effective memory aids for revision

- For nearly all students some help on how to lay out the letters so they fit onto a page is necessary

- For differentiation give the less able students shorter words and offer a bank of images to support them as well as plenty of previous examples for guidance and inspiration. Pupils' work from the previous year can be given to them to help them come up with ideas. Ask more able students to generate their own images and decode their partner's titles

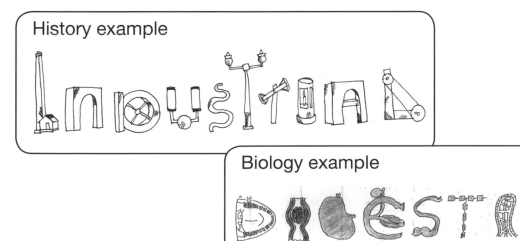

History example

Biology example

Why it works so well

- This is a fantastic activity for developing evaluative skills, especially those that focus on the most important issues

- Card sorts allow for quick and easy re-sorting and classifying

- This activity provides an opportunity to write additional information on the back of the cards

- It is also a great way to incorporate images

What to do

- Identify between three and sixteen factors that you want the students to focus on

- Students write each of these factors on a Show-me Board® and place the boards on a table

- Students arrange the boards in a pyramid shape with the most important one at the top, two in the middle and the least important three at the bottom

- Students have to justify their choice of what goes at the top. It is like a balloon debate but with no balloon!

Summary

- A superb card sorting activity that focuses on prioritisation and evaluation skills

- The Show-me Boards® provide an ideal opportunity for students to write their justification for their choices on the reverse side. Groups can then hold up their boards to compare their reasons. Ask them 'Do your reasons for putting X at the top match any another groups?' (They need to write in large letters for this to work.)

- You will need to supply plenty of content to enable students to justify their choices otherwise their explanations will be rather limited

- For differentiation tell the less able students which factor to put at the top, but then ask them to tell you why it should go there. Ask the more able to make a case for placing each factor at the top so they are forced to adapt their justification for each one

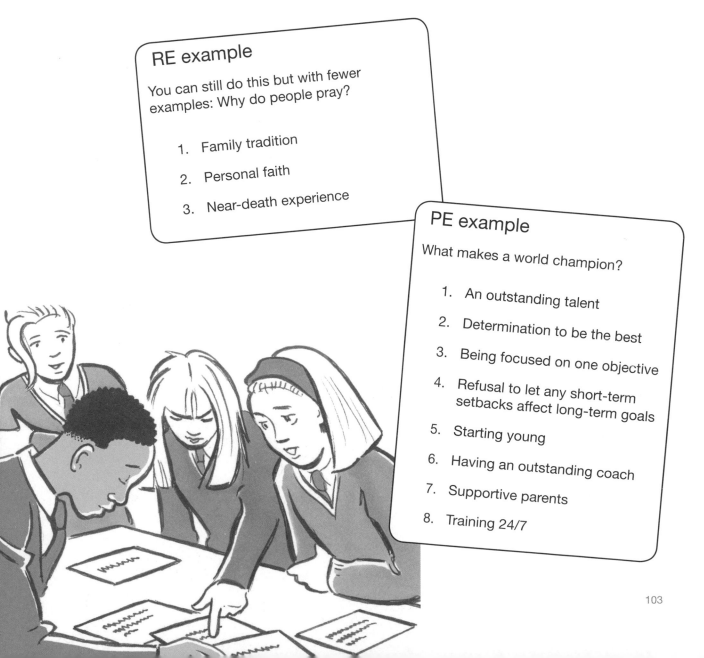

RE example

You can still do this but with fewer examples: Why do people pray?

1. Family tradition

2. Personal faith

3. Near-death experience

PE example

What makes a world champion?

1. An outstanding talent

2. Determination to be the best

3. Being focused on one objective

4. Refusal to let any short-term setbacks affect long-term goals

5. Starting young

6. Having an outstanding coach

7. Supportive parents

8. Training 24/7

18 **Silent Movies**

Why it works so well

- This activity forces students to think, participate and articulate

- Students are very media savvy these days so the majority really enjoy this sort of activity

- Be warned: some shy students or those who find it very difficult to express themselves well may want to opt out as the activity has the potential to make them look 'silly'

- It is up to you to decide if you want to let students opt out or whether you gently encourage them to have a go

What to do

- Show a ten minute film clip to the students

- Tell the students to take notes during the clip

- Give the students several minutes to order and fine tune their notes to form a continuous narration for the film

- Students move from individual work to pairs, then fours. They compare their notes with a partner and then in a four, and make a note of anything the others have included which they have missed

- Show the clip a second time but turn the volume off

- Ask students to come to the front and, in turn, offer a commentary for the film (one student per thirty seconds of the clip)

- The teacher pauses the film every thirty seconds and the next student takes over giving the commentary from the first

Summary

- This is an effective teaching strategy that increases the memory retention of students. A small change in use yields massive benefits

- This activity is an ideal way to maximise the 'perfect' film clip

- Students are not told if or when they will be required to give their one minute presentation so this should keep all the class on-task

- All students must be attentive and concentrate on their own narration

- This activity provides excellent practice for developing oral and presentation skills

- Get the rest of the class to spot any omissions or errors whilst the presenters are giving their narration

- For differentiation ask the less able students to work and present in twos or threes, the more able students can be assigned a section of the video with more challenging content, more dialogue and more demanding context

DT example

A clip showing how to set up and safely use a lathe.

English example

The scene in *Macbeth* where Lady Macbeth persuades Macbeth to kill Duncan the King.

19 Snowballing

Why it works so well

- If a picture can say a thousand words then a film clip can write a book!

- In our opinion, the ability to show students exactly what we want with a well chosen film clip is the single most significant change in education in the last ten years

- However, you need to make sure the students get the most out of the clip and this activity is definitely one way of ensuring that the students really do focus

- Short film clips are now easily available using an internet video search

What to do

- Invite students to watch a section of the video clip, which should last no more than ten minutes

- Instruct students to just watch the clip – there is no need for note taking whilst they are watching

- When the minute clip has finished, invite the students to write down three bullet points based on what they have remembered from the clip

- Students then double up with a partner to compare their points and add any new ones to their list. Then they go into fours and then eights so that they keep adding additional points to their list

Summary

- This is another activity aimed at getting the most out of a good clip because so often the students watch a video and then say they can't remember a thing about it!

- An excellent follow-up activity would be to ask the students to classify their bullet points according to themes

- The list of bullet points usually grows to about thirty after only ten minutes of video viewing. This then presents an ideal starting point for them to write up the content of the video in class or for homework

- For differentiation give the less able students a shorter clip to remember or fewer bullet points to write. You could also put reminder words on the board for them. Encourage more able students to write more detailed bullet points

Food Technology example

Show a video clip demonstrating the process of the industrial production of bread from the basic ingredients to the finished product. Some bread producers offer free videos to schools.

Geography example

Show a video of the possible effects of global warming from an organisation such as Greenpeace.

20 Songs

Why it works so well

- Most of us like a good tune and lyrics can be very easy to remember

- It is not really the music that is important here – it is the words

- This is another example of moving information from one format to another (i.e. comedy)!

What to do

- Identify a song that the students enjoy

- Replace the lyrics of a popular song with new lyrics based on the curriculum content

- Students sing the song! Year 7 may be up for this but Year 11 may be 'too cool for school' and reluctant to join in, so allow them to do this with a dose of irony whilst you sing the main bit!

- Encourage them to incorporate facts, opinions and reasons into their song

Summary

- Some students love a song, so why not focus on singing for learning? It is great fun to get the students to join in

- Lessons can be unnecessarily disruptive due to students taking ages to decide on a song, so speed up the process by setting this as a homework. The best songs can then be performed in class. Let them make their own backing tracks with a human drum-beat

- This provides a great opportunity for a *Stars in Their Eyes* type of activity

- The song itself is utterly unimportant as the real purpose of the activity is to get the students to play around with the information, which is what engenders a more challenging learning experience

- For differentiation ask less able students to create one verse each or ask them to be backing singers. Ask the more able students to be the lyricists for the whole song

Food Technology example

The Food Poisoning Song
(to the tune of 'My Old Man's a Dustman')

My old man's a fast food cook
He wears a long tall hat,
He never puts food in the freezer
So his customers never get fat.

Listeria in his chickens
Salmonella in his fowls
After a visit to his café
You'll have big problems with your bowels.

So listen all you diners
And take heed of what I say
Avoid my dad's toxic cooking
Or be sick, day after day.

21 Speed Dating

Why it works so well

- This is a short, snappy activity that involves students asking questions as well as answering them

- The repetitive element of this exercise makes recall of the questions high

- It is a great way to focus on key definitions

- The activity can be done at the end of lessons to check recall

- New words can be learned when this is used as a starter activity

What to do

- Write a series of questions on a set of cards (a maximum of seven) and on the reverse side write the answers. To ensure all students have a card it will be necessary to have a few copies of the same question

- Students are given a card as they enter the classroom. They circulate and in pairs they ask each other what the question is on their cards

- Student A asks student B their question. If student B doesn't know the answer student A reads it out to student B. Student B then reads out their question, to which Student A says they don't know the answer. Student B then reads out the answer. The two students swap their cards. They take their new cards to a new partner and continue the process. Encourage the students to make as many swaps as possible within a four minute time frame

- Allow enough time so that each student comes across all of the questions

- Allow students to guess the answers only if they have heard the question previously

Summary

- Repetition forces high recall of key definitions

- This is a simple but effective strategy that forces students to recall definitions of key language by simply having to repeat the definition many times

- It is an effective and fun revision activity that can be used several times a term

- The teacher needs to gauge the difficulty of the questions so that the less able can engage in the task whilst the more able are challenged too. One way of achieving this would be to colour-code the cards according to the level of difficulty of the questions, so certain students only pair up with students with the same colour card

- Another differentiation strategy is for less able students to repeat each question several times to their partner. Also give them questions that are fact-based and very short. Ensure that the questions for your more able students test the application of new ideas to new concepts as well as simple facts and definitions

Science example

Q. Who invented the light bulb?
A. Thomas Edison.

Q. Who invented the TV?
A. John Logie Baird.

Q. Who invented the telephone?
A. Alexander Graham Bell.

History example

Q. Who invented steam power?
A. James Watt.

Q. Who invented the telegraph?
A. Samuel Morse.

Q. Who discovered radioactivity?
A. Henri Becquerel.

22 Triangles

Why it works so well

- This is a fantastic way to get students to look carefully at lots of questions and answers at the same time

- This is a longer activity that the students can really sink their teeth into

- Not only is it a great way to revise or recap a topic but it is also an effective way to teach a new topic (i.e. give them a textbook or access to the internet and they find the answers!)

What to do

- Compose forty questions and the corresponding forty answers

- Insert each question into the grid with the answer adjacent to it (Tarsia Boards are free to download from Hermitech Laboratory at www.mmlsoft.com)

- Insert twelve 'red herring' answers around the edges

- Photocopy enough copies of the finished grid to give each group or table their own set. Laminate these and cut up the triangles making sure each set of triangles is stored separately in an envelope or plastic folder

- Students have to piece together the jigsaw to form the completed hexagon, making sure that each question is paired up with the correct answer

Summary

- This card sorting activity is enjoyably addictive if it is presented in a manageable form

- It is a fantastic way of recapping a previous topic or introducing a new subject for the first time

- Give students a time limit to complete the jigsaw – this will add to their motivation and appeals to the competitive instinct of boys in particular. The countdown clock on the IWB is perfect for this. Set a time limit or allow them to stop if they can't finish it

- An effective extension activity is to get students to find the answer (or question) to each of the twelve red herrings on the outer edges of the hexagon

- Include images in the centre of the cards for extra support/visual help

- You could give the students a hexagon grid on a topic they haven't covered yet – simply offer them a textbook and off they go!

- Always number your triangles on the back to make it easier to check that all the cards are there. Also, if one is missing, you will know exactly which one it is

- For differentiation give the less able students the cards in three stages – a packet for each stage (e.g. give them the middle six triangles first, the top nine next and then, lastly, the bottom nine – essentially you create a pack within a pack). You can also colour code to differentiate or to help identify themes (e.g. one side is red, another green and the other blue). Encourage the more able students to attempt to piece together all the cards in one go and make the concepts and words on their cards more difficult

continued

Triangles - continued

Literacy example

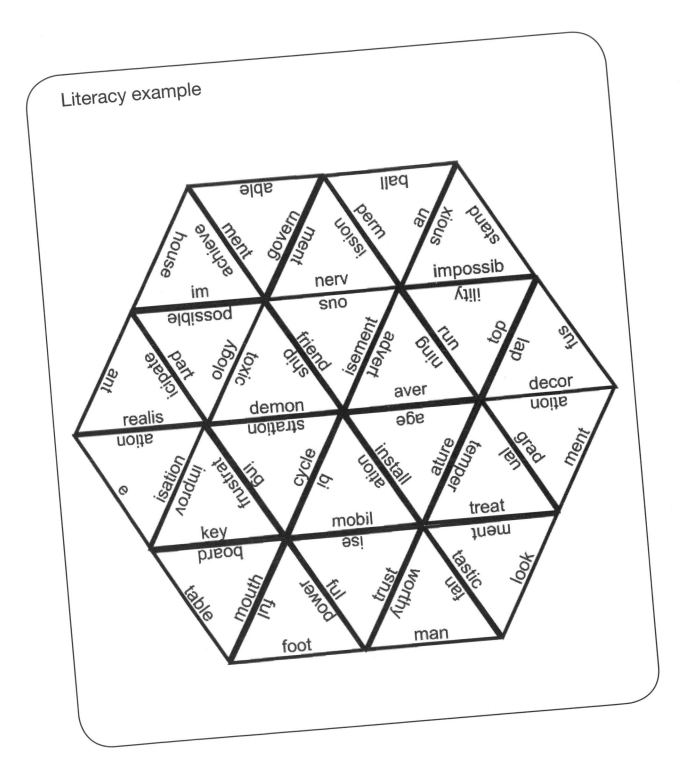

Food Technology example

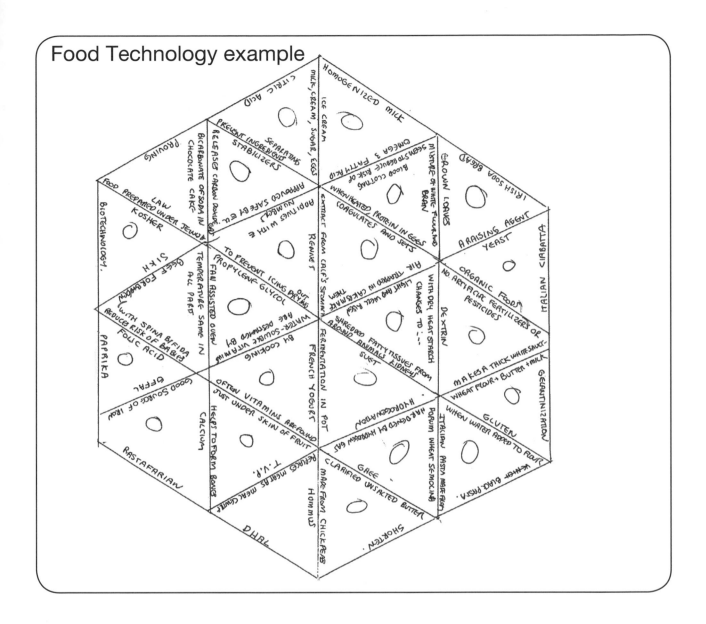

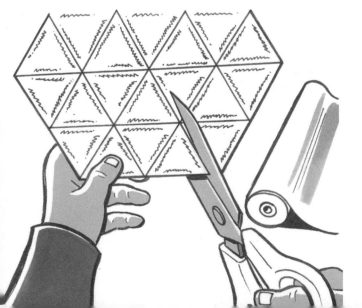

23 Word 'Splat'

Why it works so well

- For rapid-fire checking of key words and definitions this works brilliantly – if a little noisy!

- This activity creates a lot of energy in the lesson

- It can work well with any age group or subject content

- It allows the really extroverted pupils to shine and take a high profile

What to do

- The teacher places ten to twenty key terms on a poster

- Sufficient copies of the poster are required to cater for every group of students

- Position the posters around the classroom. The teacher asks a question and asks one student to go and place their hand on the correct word on the poster. This involves students getting up out of their chairs, so classroom management is an issue and you need to be confident you can control the class

- The first student to slap their hand on a correct word is given two points. Any other correct answers are given one point

Summary

- A starter or plenary activity that encompasses team work, key terminology and high energy. A great motivator!

- If posters are stuck on windows issue students with fly swatters to prevent broken glass!

- In large classes ask a student to read out the questions and the first person to put their hand up and answer correctly wins

- For differentiation give less able students a longer time to respond to the question and find the answer. Ask more able students questions focused on ideas or concepts rather than simply spotting the correct noun. Answers could also be concept-based requiring more sophisticated explanations

English example

Students are in groups and one student is asked to stand. The teacher reads out the definitions of the terms below and the student who is standing up has to react quickly, go to the nearest poster and slap their hand on the correct term. The team surrounding that student can shout out which word they think is correct and that he or she should 'splat'. The winning team is the one who slaps the correct word first.

- Alliteration
- Novel
- Adverb
- Adjective
- Onomatopoeia

Maths example

Quadrilateral splat:

- Rectangle
- Kite
- Diamond
- Rhombus
- Parallelogram
- Square
- Arrow head

Excellent Thomas, two points.

24 Seven Monkeys

Why it works so well

- This is a classic memory retention exercise

- The best way to really utilise this technique is to ensure that pupils find as many different ways of learning about the topic as possible such as making, drawing, doing and saying

- This activity suits all kinds of learners as the processes of learning the knowledge are so varied

- It offers the opportunity for creativity

What to do

- Students read the text either from the board or a sheet

- Take the text away and then in pairs the students try to remember as much as they can. They take it in turns to reveal what they remember

- Read the text to the students slowly and whilst they are listening they draw pictures or diagrams to represent the information in the text (think hieroglyphics!)

- Once you've finished the text the students decode and discuss their pictures with a partner. They can add in anything they've missed that their partner has included

- You read out the text again and they write the key words next to the appropriate picture. The teacher then says what the key words are and the students write them down

- The students have a last chance to decode their pictures and add in details by moving into fours

- Repeat the first stage so they can have one last check that they've not missed anything

Summary

- This activity sits comfortably in the mid section of a lesson and is a superb way to get students to interact with a text

- This can be your stock lesson as it is simple and very effective

- Appropriate text selection is vital – longer and/or more complex texts should be chosen for older students

- This can work well when resources are scarce. For example, you could build the whole lesson around a single textbook, with the teacher reading aloud from a key section of the book

- For differentiation offer less able students a sheet of prepared images. The students then select the most appropriate ones. More able students can try more technical terms or get them to read from a page and convert it themselves, without you having to read out the words

English example

Lear, the aging king of Britain, decides to step down from the throne and divide his kingdom evenly among his three daughters. First, however, he puts his daughters through a love test, asking each to tell him how much she loves him. Goneril and Regan, Lear's older daughters, give their father flattering answers. But Cordelia, Lear's youngest and favourite daughter, remains silent, saying that she has no words to describe how much she loves her father. Lear flies into a rage and disowns Cordelia. The king of France, who has courted Cordelia, says that he still wants to marry her even without her land, and she accompanies him to France without her father's blessing.

DT example

Screen printing is a printing technique that uses a woven mesh to support an ink-blocking stencil. The attached stencil forms open areas of mesh that transfer ink or other printable materials which can be pressed through the mesh as a sharp-edged image onto a substrate. A roller or squeegee is moved across the screen stencil, forcing or pumping ink past the threads of the woven mesh in the open areas.

Screen printing is also a stencil method of print making in which a design is imposed on a screen of silk or other fine mesh, with blank areas coated with an impermeable substance, and ink is forced through the mesh onto the printing surface.

Venn Diagrams

Why it works so well

- This is the most effective tool possible for identifying similarities and differences – and they are fantastically visual!

- This activity allows students to look at change and continuity

- An example of the theory of opposites where a 'techie' approach can be used in 'arty' subjects

- This is a common mathematical tool but is used less often in arty subjects

What to do

- Students are given a Venn diagram with two or three interlocking circles. Each circle is labelled with the name of a certain category

- Students are given a range of objects, items, terms or ideas that may or may not relate to one of these categories

- Students select each named item and place it in the most appropriate place on the Venn diagram. They can either place it in one circle if it fits that specific category only. Or they might place it where two circles overlap if the item fits into two categories. If the item fits into all three categories, then they place the word in the centre of the Venn diagram where all three circles overlap

Summary

- This activity demands skills in classification, justification, prioritisation and subject knowledge

- You can have two or three circles in each Venn diagram

- Make sure the list of items you have given them covers the topic area required

- If possible get them to do the activity first, then you teach the topic afterwards

- This is a good example of an activity that you can do with them first and then, once they have got the idea, the students can construct their own

- You can make these very easily on an IWB by simply inserting circle shapes and overlapping them

- For differentiation give less able students fewer items and make the items objects and give the more able more items and choose concepts or ideas rather than objects

- For Gifted and Talented students you could try giving them the Venn diagram with the answers already placed in the circles, but without the category headings written by each circle. They then have to work out the categories, which makes this a really challenging activity

PE example

Player, Spectator or Official:

A Needs thorough knowledge of the rules

B Needs to try to stop bad behaviour by spectators

C Needs to be fair and impartial

D Needs to have a positive attitude

E Needs to be resilient after setbacks

F Needs to be in good physical condition

G Needs to be loyal to the team

H Needs good eyesight

I Needs authority to command respect

J Needs to work against the bad behaviour of players

K Needs to plan their diet

L Needs to be firm and decisive

M Needs to offer support during bad times

N Needs to follow the instructions of their superiors

Business Studies example

Sole Trader, Partnership or Company:

A Group of lawyers

B Ice cream van salesman

C Supermarket

D Farm

E Estate agent

F Cinema

G Airline

H Restaurant

I Car repair garage

J Coach firm

K Taxi business

L Farm cooperative

M Pushbike manufacturer

N McDonald's

O A group of dentists

P The Body Shop business

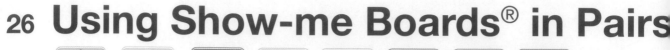

26 Using Show-me Boards® in Pairs

Why it works so well

- The biggest advantage of this activity is that it forces every student to take part

- It also allows the teacher to get into the heads of all the pupils

- It offers the opportunity for quiet pupils to shine

- The activity acts as a useful classroom management technique to settle overenthusiastic pupils

What to do

- Students are given one Show-me Board® each and put into pairs to work together

- Each pair is told to write on their boards the two topic areas that you are going to test them on

- The teacher shares some knowledge or information with the students

- Students are then asked to hold up the board which best reflects the theme that is being explored, or they can hold up both boards if both are relevant or no board if neither match up with the theme

Summary

- This activity provides a highly successful means of getting students to demonstrate that they understand themes. They reveal their understanding by holding up a board to show which theme they think they are learning about

- If you are short of Show-me Boards®, plain A4 paper works just as well

- In the longer term you might consider using laminated card so that you can make bespoke cards for each particular topic, but boards work just as well

- Dry-wipe pens have a high currency value so make sure you count them in and count them out! Have twenty numbered pens and set aside enough time to collect them in

- This is an excellent way of ensuring the whole class is engaged in an activity

- For differentiation offer less able students one board or they can work in pairs with two boards. More able students can create their own activities to test the teacher or each other

French example (can be used with all subjects)

Each pair of students must write 'spelling' on one of their boards and 'grammar' on the other board. The teacher then writes ten sentences on the whiteboard at the front of the classroom for all to see. The teacher reads out these sentences one at a time and asks the students to reveal if they have spotted a spelling mistake or a grammar mistake by holding up either the 'spelling' or the 'grammar' board. Sometimes you can put both mistakes into a sentence and then the students can legitimately hold up both boards! Equally, it is good to include some sentences with no mistakes so that the students, when asked, don't hold up either of their boards.

Geography example

Show a film clip from the opening scenes of any James Bond film (usually a car chase sequence). Ask the pupils to write 'physical geography' on one board and 'human geography' on the other. At various points during the film clip, simply pause the video and invite the pupils to show what type of geography they have just seen (i.e. physical, human or both) and then ask them to elaborate on what it is they have observed by writing some notes under the appropriate heading on the board itself.

27 Word Memory Game

Why it works so well

- Films and diagrams are highly visual whereas this activity gets students to work with text which is harder

- It assumes the sum of the parts is greater than what pupils can recall individually

- Listening to others often reminds pupils of things they have forgotten

- This activity values all contributions

What to do

- Students are given a piece of text or an image

- Ask them to try to remember as much of it as possible

- After a short period of time (1–2 minutes) go round the class and ask the students to share one thing they can remember from the image or text

- The teacher writes these on the board and the class copy all the points into their books

- If the students don't have much information then let them read the text or look at the image again

- Try to keep the momentum going in the lesson as pace is the key here

Summary

- This activity demands good memory recall and forces the pupils to look closely at text

- This is a great way to work with an important image or piece of text which may be needed for future revision

- Set some rules, such as no hesitation or delay and that they must speak up so others can hear

- Keep up the pace in this lesson. You could invite students to come up to the front and write their list on the board

- This can be effective as a group activity where groups compete with each other

- For differentiation invite your least able students to start the list or subtly help them if needed. Choose more able students to supply information towards the end of the activity

English example

Remembering the key aspects of Act 1 of *King Lear*:

- Shakespeare's dark tragedy *King Lear* opens with the fictional king of England, King Lear, handing over his kingdom to his daughters, Regan and Goneril, whom he believes truly love him. Lear intends to stay with each daughter consecutively, accompanied by one hundred loyal knights.

- Angry that Cordelia, his youngest daughter, does not appear to love him as do Goneril and Regan, Lear banishes Cordelia and the Earl of Kent, the servant who attempts to defend her. Cordelia leaves and is taken by the King of France as his Queen.

- Edmund, the loved but illegitimate son of the Earl of Gloucester, plots to have his elder brother Edgar's reputation ruined. Edmund tricks Gloucester into believing that Edgar wanted to kill him.

- The disrespectful Goneril conspires to have Lear driven out of her house.

- Kent, who has now disguised his identity to serve Lear, earns the king's respect by defending his name. Goneril offends Lear and dismisses fifty of his knights. Lear starts to realise Cordelia was not so disrespecting. He decides to leave for Regan's home, where he feels sure he will be treated properly.

- Lear instructs Kent to deliver several letters to Gloucester. The Fool teaches Lear several riddles.

PE example

Remembering the dimensions of a hockey pitch:

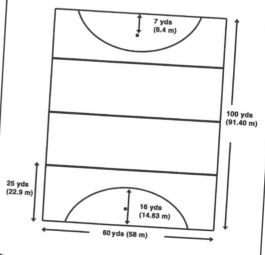

28 Stand Up/Sit Down

Why it works so well

- It allows easy checking of what is known and not known

- Pupils are still learning even though they are sitting down

- The pupils left at the end can 'show off' by revealing what the rest of the class didn't remember

- A good way to end a lesson well

What to do

- Ask the students to write on their Show-me Boards® some information relating to a specific topic (e.g. famous artists, composers, irregular verbs). The students must keep what they have written on the board 'hidden'

- Make sure the topic is absolutely clear by clarifying the focus (e.g. Is it a fact or a date or a person or an opinion that the student has written down?)

- All the students then stand up, keeping their boards hidden and the teacher tries to guess what is on their boards by calling out some possible answers

- If what the teacher has said corresponds with what the students have written on their board, they must sit down, making sure they reveal what is written on their board before they do so

- Once you have run out of ideas ask individual students to reveal the information on their boards and if this matches the information on another student's board then they too must sit down

- The winner is the last student(s) left standing

Summary

- This activity gets the whole class involved and is a good recap activity as well as providing an opportunity for your brightest pupils to shine

- A superb da Vinci moment as there is little fuss, everyone is involved and it is easy to monitor

- Keep up the pace by encouraging students to write their words rapidly and to sit down quickly

- A brilliant follow-up activity is to suggest themes (or they can come up with their own) and they then organise their ideas into lists under each themed heading

- Invite a student up to the front of the classroom to call out the possible answers so that the whole activity becomes student centred

- For differentiation ask less able students to start the list and choose the more able students towards the end of the activity

Music example

You have just done some work on orchestras so the students reflect on this work. Some might have written examples of instruments played in an orchestra, or the type of music played, or how many people are in an orchestra, or names of composers who have written music for the orchestra.

Well done William - you're the last one standing, you've won!

Food Technology example

The students are reflecting on making a cake. Some have written about ingredients, others on the processes involved (weighing and measuring) and others on how it felt to eat the cake!

What's the Question?

Why it works so well

- This activity inverts the classic comprehension question

- It is much harder to generate a question than simply to guess the right answer

- It saves a lot of teacher preparation but is more powerful than designing time consuming comprehension questions

- Increasing the number of different questions increases the level of challenge

What to do

- Give the pupils a word or phrase and tell them this is the answer (e.g. photosynthesis)

- They have to generate a question that will produce the closed response 'photosynthesis'

- Invite them to interrogate a textbook or whatever material it is you are using to work out their questions

- Ask them to try to create as many questions as possible (the first one is the easiest to come up with, whereas the third or fourth question gets a lot harder!)

Summary

- This is a reverse of the traditional comprehension question and really gets the pupils to think hard. What's more, it is not that easy to do!

- Make sure you use answers that could generate more than one question

- Demonstrate how to do this activity at the start of the lesson to avoid any confusion

- Ask the pupils to write their questions on a Show-me Board® so that you can compile their questions into a list for later use

- For differentiation generate one question for less able students or use a fill-in-the-gap type exercise to help them get started, where they just have to provide the missing word(s). Encourage more able students to formulate as many questions as they can so it becomes increasingly challenging

Music example

This provides a really effective method for working with a textbook

- When you start to increase the number of questions they must find, the students really have to draw on a lot more detail and a wider range of knowledge in order to do this

- This can work well in groups by setting them in competition with each other to come up with the most questions

- Repeat the exercise in a few weeks time to see if they can remember the list they created and to check it really embeds into their memory

Science example

Pupils have been given two pages of a textbook to read in readiness for the lesson on photosynthesis. The teacher simply invites the class to think up between one and five questions that would generate the answer 'photosynthesis' (e.g. What is the process called where sunlight shines onto plants to create oxygen?)

Why it works so well

- This activity is a great way to use the ICT suite and get students to create their own card sets which can be recycled the following year

- This activity can be used as a revision exercise but it also extremely effective for imparting knowledge in the first instance

- Due to the competitive element, students will happily play this and will be learning along the way

What to do

- Students are given an identical sets of trump cards
- One student selects a category, reads out the value and sees if their score is higher than their partner's
- If it is higher, then they take their partner's card and their own and put both to the bottom of their pile
- The winner of each round gets to choose the next category, which might be the same one or a different category
- The first player to take all their partner's cards wins

Summary

- This activity provides an excellent way of getting students to remember facts without even realising it!

- Out of all the educational games available to teachers to use in the classroom, this is probably the most effective

- Change values halfway through the game (e.g. lowest value for x now wins)

- Do not be afraid to move away from just using facts – subjective analysis can make for the best discussions

- For a whole class version you can attempt 'Play Your Cards Right', where they call out 'higher' or 'lower'

- Include some additional details in the categories to develop their knowledge. For differentiation give less able students fewer cards to make this activity slightly easier. This exercise particularly suits the more able who can include some value categories in their cards as well as facts and details (e.g. importance or significance) and then ask them to justify their decision

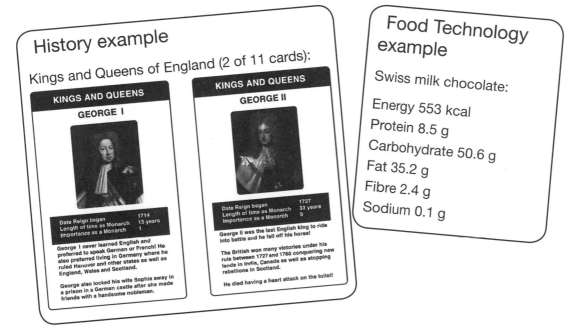

History example

Kings and Queens of England (2 of 11 cards):

KINGS AND QUEENS
GEORGE I

Date Reign began 1714
Length of time as Monarch 13 years
Importance as a Monarch 1

George I never learned English and preferred to speak German or French! He also preferred living in Germany where he ruled Hanover and other states as well as England, Wales and Scotland.

George also locked his wife Sophia away in a prison in a German castle after she made friends with a handsome nobleman.

KINGS AND QUEENS
GEORGE II

Date Reign began 1727
Length of time as Monarch 33 years
Importance as a Monarch 9

George II was the last English king to ride into battle and he fell off his horse!

The British won many victories under his rule between 1727 and 1760 conquering new lands in India, Canada as well as stopping rebellions in Scotland.

He died having a heart attack on the toilet!

Food Technology example

Swiss milk chocolate:

Energy 553 kcal
Protein 8.5 g
Carbohydrate 50.6 g
Fat 35.2 g
Fibre 2.4 g
Sodium 0.1 g

I've won all the cards - I've won the game!

31 Relational Diagrams

Why it works so well

- Students are asked to classify information which improves thinking skills

- Provides a fantastic way of looking at similarity and/or difference

- Avoids lots of writing

- Targets what they know quickly and clearly

What to do

- Give the students a list of words and ask them to put them in circles on a relational diagram

- This can be done with objects and images as well as words

- Do this after they have mastered the Venn diagram (Activity 25), but remember that this is used in different circumstances when a Venn diagram won't work

Summary

- This activity is an excellent way of getting students to show relationships between a series of items. However, unlike in the Venn diagram exercise, it can be used for items that are related but where there is no overlap, as shown by the intersection on a Venn diagram

- A great way to use ICT (through an IWB or projector) for auto shapes and images

- It can be a fantastic physical activity using a hula hoop or string in the shape of a circle if you want to do a lively version!

- For differentiation give less able students fewer words and fill in some of the circles to get them started. Provide more able students with more information and little or no help with what goes where. Ask them to justify their choice

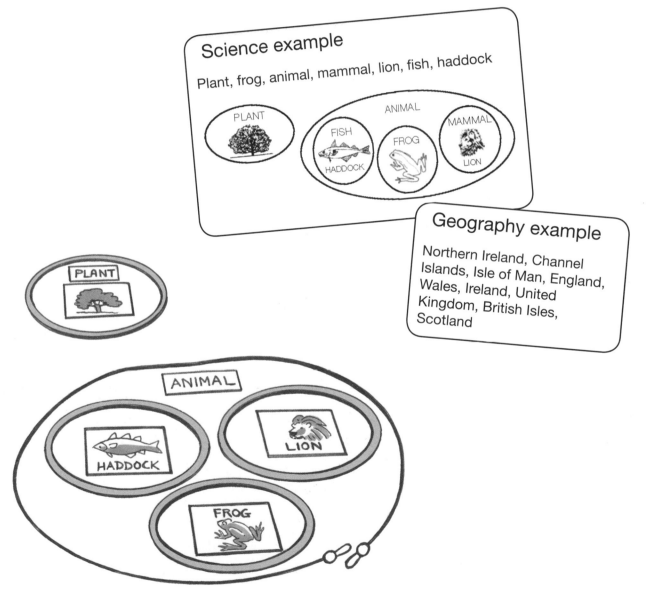

32 Spot the Odd One Out – With a Difference!

Why it works so well

- This is a detailed activity that forces students to look at the key language carefully

- It allows for easy differentiation because the teacher can simply increase the number of variables on which the pupils focus

- It allows for other easy-to-apply teaching activities such as pairs games and bingo

What to do

- Students copy from the board so no preparation is needed! The grid can also be prepared in advance and photocopied

- The grid has thirty key terms or numbers on it

- The teacher offers sets of four values with one being the odd one out

- In pairs the students choose which one is the odd one out

Summary

- This activity helps to embed key language in the students' memory as well as testing understanding. It focuses upon the key vocabulary that all exam boards indicate is essential to achieving the highest marks

- This activity should replace the word search which we believe should be banned from secondary education!

- It is low on preparation (especially if the students make them) but still a great way to keep focusing on the same material for reinforcement

- It can be a fantastic physical activity using pupils in role (e.g. Cyril Circle describes his properties before the students go on to decide which is the odd one out)

- You can get the students to make their own!

- For differentiation give less able students fewer choices and focus on the easiest ones. Ask more able students to add to the list of four but keep the same odd one out. They can make more 'sets' themselves

Maths examples

Which is the odd one out from the following list:

1	Circle	11	Area	21	Triangle
2	Multiply	12	Parallelogram	22	Minus
3	Obtuse angle	13	60	23	Rectangle
4	360	14	Right angle	24	Diameter
5	Add	15	3	25	Acute angle
6	180	16	Square	26	4
7	Divide	17	Line	27	Venn diagram
8	Sphere	18	Equilateral	28	Reflex angle
9	Quadrilateral	19	Circumference	29	Cube
10	90	20	Pyramid	30	Root

Which is the odd one out from the following list:

a) 1, 12, 16, 23
b) 6, 10, 13, 15
c) 2, 7, 24, 29
d) 9, 12, 21, 27
e) 3, 14, 25, 28
f) 1, 11, 19, 24

33 Option-Based Learning

Why it works so well

- This activity gives students the opportunity to experiment in their learning

- It solves the age old problem of asking students questions in class: what's the point of asking students a question if they already know the answer? Equally, what's the point of asking a question if they don't know the answer?

- It encourages pupils to consider issues from multiple perspectives and to make decisions

- The teacher addresses all the different possible answers and why certain answers are incorrect

What to do

- Students are offered a variety of potentially valid answers to a question

- They are challenged to justify which one they think is best and why

- The teacher does have a 'best' answer, if possible

- The class is given enough information to help them work out which one is best

Summary

- This activity is a brilliant way of exploring the validity of different responses to a given dilemma

- It also gets the students to examine different possibilities and to prioritise the validity of evidence

- Don't reveal the answer immediately but explore all possibilities in depth. The answer should not be given away until every option has been explored. Do not rush!

- Allow students enough time to change their minds

- Make sure there is proper consolidation afterwards so you arrive at the correct answer in the end

Music example

You are composing a piece of music which describes a thunderstorm. Which of the following instrumental combinations will most successfully represent the sound of a thunderstorm?

1. Oboe, timpani, bassoon, piano

2. Violin, cello, harp, glockenspiel

3. Double bass, harp, acoustic guitar, drum kit

4. Cymbals, viola, trombone, saxophone

Drama example

In miming throwing and catching a ball, which one of the following is the most important skill that mime artists will need to throw the ball back and forth to each other?

1. Facial expressions

2. Over-exaggeration

3. Normal actions then freeze-frame

4. Good use of floor space

Thunder.

Excellent!

34 Carousel

Why it works so well

- A superb way of catering for different learning styles as well as making lessons powerful and multi-sensory

- Approaching a topic from so many different angles really helps the students to gain a more in depth understanding of a topic

- This is a really fun activity and students love the variety of approaches

- It creates a real buzz in the classroom – and gives you an excuse to use a whistle!

What to do

- Students are divided into small groups but there must be seven groups, so class size will dictate how many students are in each group

- The seven stations will be: a word station, picture station, body station, music station, people station, self station and number station

- These seven work stations are located around the room (see example below)

- The class get five minutes at each work station to complete the given task

- After each five minute session the class move on to the next station, hence the term 'carousel' which is often used to describe this type of activity

- After thirty-five minutes the carousel stops and consolidation work is carried out

Summary

- This activity provides an effective means of exploring the different ways we can learn about the same topic

- The more we look at a topic from different angles, the more likely we are to understand it

- Always ensure that the task to be completed at each station focuses on what you want them to learn

- For differentiation utilise your learning support assistant to help less able groups or assign stronger students to work with the weaker ones. Ask more able students to create their own stations once they have studied a particular topic

continued

Carousel - continued

Geography example

What each group will be doing at the different stations for work on volcanoes:

- Word station – pupils write down what happens when a volcano erupts whilst watching a short film clip

- Picture station – pupils copy and label a diagram of a cross section of a volcano

- Body station – pupils rearrange a jigsaw of a diagram of a cross section of a volcano

- Music station – pupils sing or listen to a song called 'The Volcano Song' (http://www.youtube.com/watch?v=BcFtpWjZwlE)

- People station – pupils listen to a volcanologist being interviewed about what causes a volcano to erupt

- Self station – pupils write a short account of what they would feel like if they were caught near an erupting volcano

- Number station – show pupils some data about volcanic eruptions and ask them to work out some averages around Richter scale averages, times of year and frequency

Five minutes later

Repeat every five minutes

Maths example

What each group will be doing at the different stations for work on the properties of triangles:

- Word station – pupils write down the properties and angles of different kinds of triangles without the use of drawings

- Picture station – pupils must correctly copy and label some different triangles

- Body station – pupils use a ball of wool to show they know the shape of different types of triangle from written descriptions

- Music station – pupils sing or listen to a song called 'My Triangle' (which James Blunt performed on *Sesame Street!*)

- People station – pupils listen to a mathematician being interviewed about what properties are found in triangles

- Self station – pupils write a short review of what they know about triangles

- Number station – show pupils some data about different triangles and they decide which type of triangle matches the data

35 Using the Spotlight Tool to Reveal a Picture

Why it works so well

- We all love a mystery. It is great fun for the students to try to work out what is underneath the spotlight

- You can invite a student to come up to the front at the end of the lesson to finally reveal the picture

- Ask the students to guess what the image is in as few an attempts as possible

- Make sure the image is quite unusual to heighten the 'ah!' factor

What to do

- All IWBs have a spotlight tool

- Select a small section of an image

- Move the spotlight around the screen

- Can the students guess what the hidden picture is?

- Choose different shapes as the reveal tool (circle, square or ellipse)

- Make the shapes larger to make it easier to guess the image

Summary

- This activity is a superb way of getting the absolute most out of a crucial diagram or image

- Focus on different parts of the image or diagram at different times whilst the pupils are trying to guess what is hidden

- Make sure you have the picture hidden first before you bring it up as a PowerPoint – it is no good if the picture pops up first and then you put on the spotlight tool!

- Make sure you know the picture well, so you can avoid revealing the bits that immediately give the answer away

- For differentiation prime less able students with clues to help them guess correctly. Offer the more able no clues, keep the shape small and move the spotlight tool more quickly

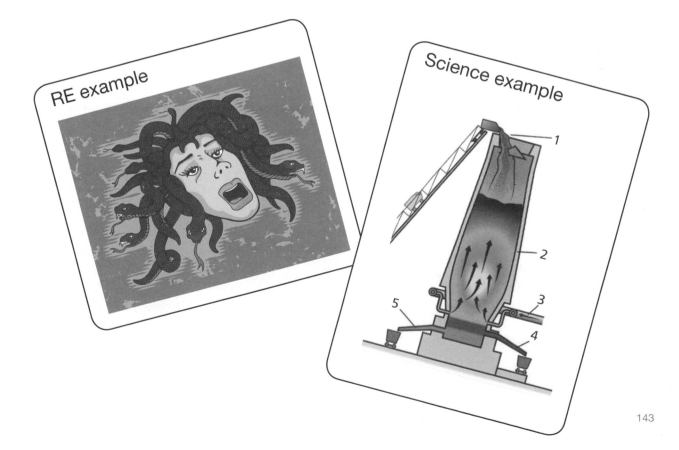

Why it works so well

- This activity gives the lesson a certain 'wow' factor

- Magic is as attractive today as it was thousands of years ago – this can add some excitement to the classroom

- Builds another one of the those 'ah!' moments which are always invaluable

- Harnesses technology in a productive and powerful way

What to do

- Divide the IWB in two and make each half a different colour

- Write a question on the right hand side in a colour that stands out against the background

- Then write the answer on the left hand side in the same colour as the background so it is 'hidden' (it is actually written over the colour)

- When you drag the question across to the right hand side of the board the answer is revealed as the text is a different colour to the background

Summary

- This activity involves an extremely cunning use of colour to create an illusion of magic!

- A great way to give a magical feeling to a lesson

- Students can create their own in a PowerPoint presentation. Nearly all IWB software is free so the students can make their own

- For differentiation prime less able students with clues to help them guess correctly and offer more able students no clues or support

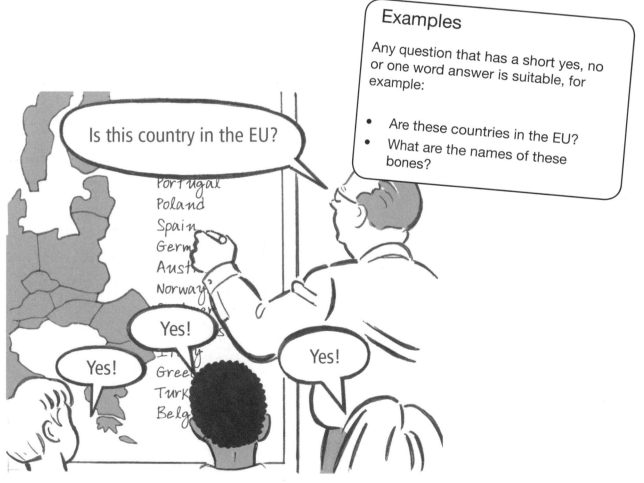

Examples

Any question that has a short yes, no or one word answer is suitable, for example:

- Are these countries in the EU?
- What are the names of these bones?

37 Mixed Doubles

Why it works so well

- This activity forces pupils to make connections instead of seeing concepts in isolation

- A whole range of activities can be harnessed from this resource such as paired activities, sequencing and classifying

- It suits very visual material as well as word or number-based work

- Low preparation but high return

What to do

- Create a numbered grid

- Place an image or a piece of text in each square

- Ask a student to select two numbers

- They have to describe or explain a connection between the two corresponding images

- Ask another student to choose two other numbers and describe the connection between the images they represent

- Continue until all images have been discussed

Summary

- This is a superb *Question of Sport* type activity that reinforces the connection between images and words

- Students can create their own in a PowerPoint presentation using the 'insert table' function

- Use a grid with just words or just pictures

- For differentiation ask less able students for one connection and encourage more able students to find more than one connection between the two images or words revealed in the first round

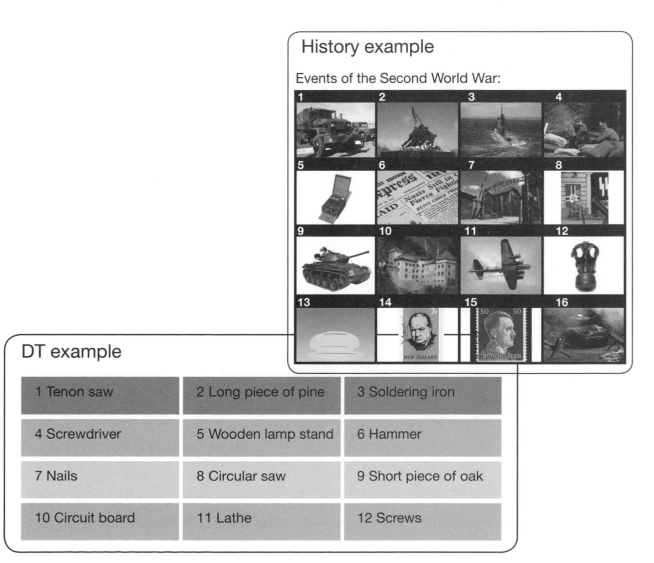

History example

Events of the Second World War:

DT example

1 Tenon saw	2 Long piece of pine	3 Soldering iron
4 Screwdriver	5 Wooden lamp stand	6 Hammer
7 Nails	8 Circular saw	9 Short piece of oak
10 Circuit board	11 Lathe	12 Screws

38 Summarising Using Shapes

Why it works so well

- It provides a well structured activity that is short and snappy

- The shapes provide an easy rationale to the students and help them to prop up their learning

- It allows for knowledge focused activities as well as understanding

- Strong on developing literacy skills

What to do

- Draw a triangle and ask the students to read a section of text, select three key facts and place one at each point of the triangle

- Draw a square with 'who' in one corner, 'what' in another, 'where' in another and 'when' in the last one

- Students then try to find information from the text which would satisfy each of the four questions

- Then draw a circle and ask the students to write one sentence that captures the section of text in one sentence

Summary

- This activity is a fantastic way of ensuring that students focus on specific elements within a piece of text

- It provides a really effective way of using the textbook to maximum effect

- The activity forces the students to process and think through the information they are reading

- The circle activity is a good evaluative activity to prove they have captured the essence of the text

- The activity may be developed further by doing a 'show and tell' with the rest of class to share more details

- For differentiation ask less able students for one answer for each element of the shapes and encourage more able students to write additional information in the corner of each shape

Art example

Three facts about Leonardo da Vinci:
1. He was a painter
2. His mother was a peasant woman
3. He lived in Florence for part of his life

Who, when, where and what?
- Who? A famous Renaissance inventor, painter and architect.
- When? He was born in 1452.
- Where? A small Tuscan town called Vinci.
- What? He was able to design catapults, portable bridges and even flying machines.

Summary:
- A genius who had one of the most brilliant and creative minds ever.

History example

Three facts about Louis Pasteur:
1. His father was a tanner.
2. He developed the germ theory of disease.
3. His body is interred beneath the Institute Pasteur in Paris in an ornate vault covered in mosaics.

Who, what, when and where?
- Who? A French chemist and microbiologist.
- When? He was born in 1822.
- Where? In Dole, in the Jura region of France.
- What? He is famous for inventing pasteurisation and made significant breakthroughs in disease prevention and vaccines.

Summary:
- A talented chemist who is now regarded as one of the main founders of microbiology.

39

Multi-Sensory Worksheet

Why it works so well

- As with all multi-sensory teaching, this has the potential to unlock doors for various students. You could argue that if they don't know what something looks, tastes and smells like then how can they imagine it? Visualisation can therefore be very effective

- If you don't tap into the whole multi-sensory approach, this activity can help to provide variety and assist with adopting multiple perspectives

What to do

- Show a film or read a section of a text

- Ask the students to identify as many things as they can under the headings of 'see', 'hear', 'taste', 'touch', 'do', 'smell' and 'feel' by imagining they are actually involved in or part of the scene/setting

Summary

- This is a powerful way of inviting the students to feel part of or involved in a scene or event

- You are almost creating a virtual field trip type experience by encouraging the pupils to reflect on what they might feel, see, touch, taste, do, smell and hear

- It works well with descriptive texts as well as film clips

- This activity is also a way to develop empathy skills

- For differentiation ask less able students to focus on what they can see and hear and ask the more able students to identify several points under each heading

SEE

TASTE

SMELL

DO

Template example

Imagine you are involved in the film.

40

Jigsaws

Why it works so well

- During this activity students have to think laterally and be very active in processing information rather than passively absorbing facts

- With pace the activity maintains the interest of the students

- It can be word or picture-based

- This activity works well with longer pieces of writing as well as short definitions or quotes

What to do

- Split up a word into individual letters, a quote into individual words, or a paragraph/essay into individual sentences

- Pass these muddled up words/quotes/paragraphs/essays to pairs or groups of students

- Simply ask them to arrange these in the right order

- Allow them to look at a textbook or other material for help

Summary

- This is a fantastic way of focusing on either key language, quotes, formulae or longer passages of text

- It is an entertaining yet challenging way of concentrating on literacy skills such as spelling, good grammar and sentence formation

- The pupils are doing more work than you!

- This activity encourages the students to create their own jigsaw tasks with a good use of sticky notes

- For differentiation encourage less able students to focus on shorter words and give more able students longer and more complex texts that deal with more challenging concepts

Examples

What do these quotations say?

appears. the is student master When ready the,

Buddhist saying

is its a everywhere. treasure will follow owner Learning that

Chinese proverb

is remembrance. All knowledge but

(Answers:

When the student is ready, the master appears.

Learning is a treasure that will follow its owner everywhere.

All knowledge is but remembrance.)

Plato

41 Probing Questions

Why it works so well

- This activity encourages students to ask questions rather than just respond to questions

- It offers an opportunity for pupils to answer their own questions

- It fosters independent thinking and processing

- It also gets pupils to think about the challenge of different kinds of questions

What to do

- The best questions can be based around the 5Ws: Who? When? Where? What? and Why?

Summary

- This activity involves asking students to reflect on a chunk of newly learnt material by using a series of probing questions

- This will develop students' ability to transfer skills from one situation to another and also their ability to draw on appropriate skills before diving into the next task

- It encourages students to learn from their mistakes and to think about their own learning

- Above all, it provides them with an opportunity to take responsibility for their own learning

- This activity encourages students to ask their own questions about a topic before they engage with the material, which is a great way to increase their independence

- For differentiation with less able students use questions that primarily ask the students to describe. For more able students base the questions on higher order thinking skills – probing questions usually ask them to evaluate or predict

Science example

Students complete an investigation into the reaction of marble chips with hydrochloric acid. One third of the class change the particle size, one third of the class change the acid temperature and the rest change the acid concentration. At the completion of the task, when the results have been produced, conclusions drawn and graphs completed, the students that made the most effective working unit are asked a series of questions. These include:

1. How did you decide to collect the gas?

2. How did you select the timings intervals for gas collection observations?

3. What factors did you consider when deciding on the number of different acid concentrations for the experiment?

4. How did you manage your time?

5. How did you reduce errors?

6. What have you discovered today that could be used to improve your investigation skills next time?

DT example

Students are split into groups of three to make a pop bottle holder. When the activity is complete they are asked a series of questions:

- What skills did you use to realise the pop bottle holder?
- What skills did you use that you could transfer to another project?
- How did you manage your time?
- How did you get on as a team?
- How did you delegate work?
- Who kept the team on-task?
- How could you have worked better as a team?

discuss the answers
these questions.

42 Spiderman

Why it works so well

- The activity allows students to classify information

- It encourages sub-strands of information to be identified

- The use of images supports long-term recall

- The activity replaces standard note taking

- This is a very creative activity

What to do

- The teacher asks the students to complete a spider diagram of a topic, as a lesson by lesson exercise

- The name of the topic goes at the centre of the page and then at the end of each lesson some time is given for the students to add a couple of key points covered in that lesson

- In this way students reflect on today's learning in relation to the whole topic

Summary

- Graphic organisers are a powerful tool to visually represent learnt knowledge and target areas where knowledge is weaker. They also allow students to extend knowledge by increasing the number of branches and connections

- This is a great opportunity for felt-tip pens to be used to make the diagrams colourful and memorable

- For differentiation give less able students a completed spider diagram without lines – the students add lines on the diagram to indicate any connections they can see. Ask more able students to colour code the spider diagram to differentiate between different themes

43 Thinking Maps

Why it works so well

- The activity helps students to master concepts and allows them to choose a technique they are happy with

- In time pupils choose the correct map for different types of thinking

- This activity supports metacognition

- A good assessment tool for the teacher to quickly identify what has and hasn't been understood

What to do

- The teacher draws a template of one of the maps for thinking

- Students decide where each piece of information should go on the map

- The students take it in turns to talk about why they have chosen the information on their map for thinking

- The teacher exlains why a particular type of map is best suited to representing a particular type of thinking (circle map for describing words that are relevant to a specific topic, e.g. mammals in the middle and other examples such as horse and cow in the outer circle)

Summary

- This is an excellent activity for getting students to focus on the key thinking processes such as sequencing, classifying, prioritising and information processing

- Each thinking map focuses on a different type of thinking such as sequencing, classifying or cause/effect

- Once the students are familiar with the concepts encourage them to choose the appropriate thinking map for a given topic

- Images can also be incorporated into the thinking maps as well as words and numbers

- The more students are exposed to these kinds of maps the better they will become at recognising for themselves why certain maps are more appropriate for certain types of thinking than others

- When discussion takes this direction the students will be entering the realms of metacognition – in other words they will be thinking about their thinking processes

- For differentiation give less able students more information and a few examples to get them started. For more able students leave all the spaces blank and ask the students to fill them in and even explain why they have chosen that particular map over others

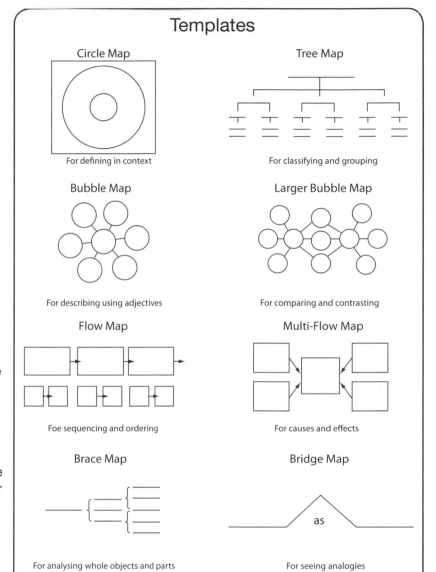

Templates

Circle Map

For defining in context

Tree Map

For classifying and grouping

Bubble Map

For describing using adjectives

Larger Bubble Map

For comparing and contrasting

Flow Map

Foe sequencing and ordering

Multi-Flow Map

For causes and effects

Brace Map

For analysing whole objects and parts

Bridge Map

as

For seeing analogies

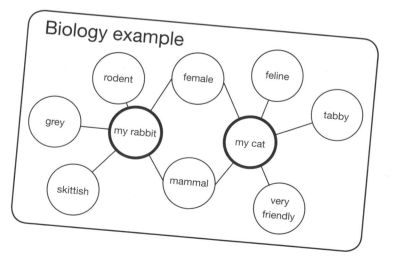

Biology example

rodent — female — feline

grey — my rabbit — tabby

skittish — mammal — my cat — very friendly

Collective Memory

Why it works so well

- This is a brilliant technique for getting pupils to engage with a diagram and really enthuse about its content

- This activity promotes good group work as pupils work as a team, not in a team

- This activity forces students to process carefully the content of a diagram

- This is a good revision tool if producing a map from memory

What to do

- The teacher divides the class into groups of four

- One student per group is the designated scribe and is assigned a pen and a Show-me Board® to write on

- Let the whole class see the diagram projected onto the IWB/OHP for one minute

- Then 'hide' the image and ask the student scribe to draw a copy of the diagram. The scribe draws but the rest of the group talk and add information that they remember

- Students are given four 'looks' at the diagram in total so repeat the process three more times

- The rule is that when the image is revealed they are not allowed to draw

Summary

- Key diagrams and the information they contain can be retained more effectively with this powerful memory activity

- Sometimes it is better to give the students a template of the diagram, particularly if it is very detailed

- Encourage the students to produce an exact copy of the diagram, including all the words, lines and images

- Create a competitive element by saying that the group that produces the closest match to the original 'wins'

- This activity is a fantastic way to make information processing more active

- For differentiation give less able students more information from the diagram on their sheet so that they have less of the diagram to remember and recreate, and for more able students leave all the spaces blank and ask the students to fill in them all

continued

Collective Memory - ^{continued}

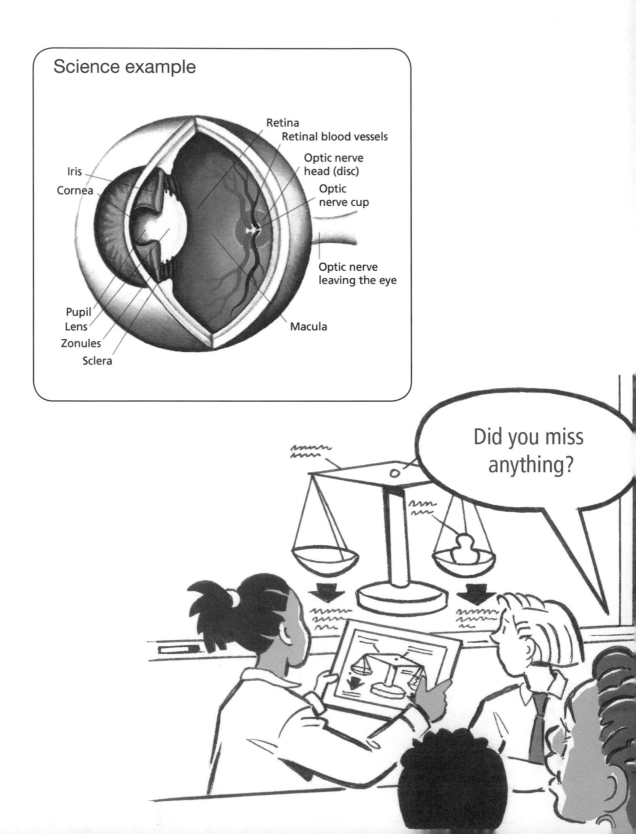

Physics example

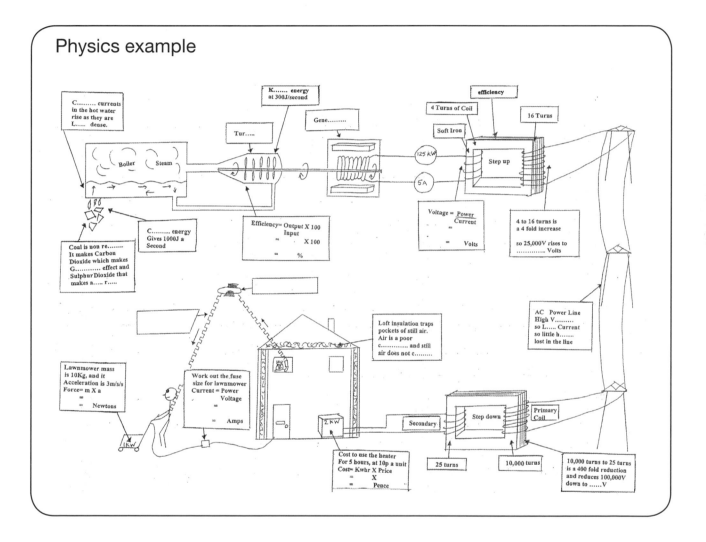

C......... currents in the hot water rise as they are L...... dense.

K....... energy at 300J/second

Gene.........

efficiency

4 Turns of Coil

16 Turns

Soft Iron

Tur.....

Boiler   Steam

125 kW

5A

Step up

Coal is non re........ It makes Carbon Dioxide which makes G............ effect and Sulphur Dioxide that makes a..... r......

C......... energy Gives 1000J a Second

Efficiency= Output X 100
          Input
       =   X 100
       =   %

Voltage = Power
          Current
        =
        =   Volts

4 to 16 turns is a 4 fold increase

so 25,000V rises to .... Volts

AC Power Line High V........ so L...... Current so little h....... lost in the line

Loft insulation traps pockets of still air. Air is a poor c............ and still air does not c........

Lawnmower mass is 10Kg, and it Acceleration is 3m/s/s Force= m X a
    =
    =   Newtons

Work out the fuse size for lawnmower Current = Power
          Voltage
        =
        =   Amps

1KW

2 KW

Secondary

Step down

Primary Coil

25 turns

10,000 turns

Cost to use the heater For 5 hours, at 10p a unit Cost= Kwhr X Price
    =   X
    =   Pence

10,000 turns to 25 turns is a 400 fold reduction and reduces 100,000V down to V

45 Alphabet Soup

Why it works so well

- This activity makes clear that the initial letter is what is required to complete the sheet

- Students do not have to start at A and work through the alphabet – they can choose any letter they know something about

- It offers clear targets rather than an open ended task

- It differentiates well by asking for different letters from different pupils

What to do

- The teacher offers a worksheet to students with the twenty-six letters of the alphabet listed vertically

- In the first column the students write a word connected with the topic under review

- In the second column they have to explain or justify why they have chosen that word

- If students are struggling on a letter they can miss that one out and come back to it later

Summary

- The letters of the alphabet provide a scaffold on which students can hang their knowledge and understanding – very clear parameters are set

- This is a great recap or revision exercise

- It could be used as an active way of working though a textbook for a new topic

- Students simply scan the textbook for key ideas and words, fill them in on the sheet and then attach some kind of context next to them

- All the information put into the 'alphabet soup' sheet can form the basis of a glossary or further classification work

- For differentiation give less able students fewer letters to complete and ask more able students to identify more than one word per letter

continued

Alphabet Soup - continued

Template

Biology example		Business Studies example

Biology example
a – antelope
b – blue shark
c – capercaillie
d – devil fish
e – Essex skipper
f – fox
g – great black-backed gull
h – horned dung beetle
i – ibex
j – jackdaw
k – knot
l – little tern
m – may bug
n – Norway lemming
o – ostrich
p – ptarmigan
q – quail
r – red grouse
s – snipe
t – termite
u – urchin
v – vole
w – water beetle
x – xanthareel
y – yak
z – zebra

LETTER	WORD
A	
B	
C	
D	
E	
F	
G	
H	
I	
J	
K	
L	
M	
N	
O	
P	
Q	
R	
S	
T	
U	
V	
W	
X	
Y	
Z	

Business Studies example

A – auditors
B – break-even
C – creditors
D – debtors
E – employees
F – fixed assets
G – gross profit
H – human resources
I – investment
J – job enrichment
K – key performance indicators
L – liabilities
M – market share
N – net income
O – opportunities
P – profit and loss statement
Q – quarters
R – revenue
S – strengths
T – threats
U – unique selling point
V – variable costs
W – weaknesses
X – x theory
Y – y theory
Z – zero-rated VAT

Part 4

The A to Z of Teaching

An alphabetically wonderful collection of insights and ideas

This is an A to Z of the things that are useful to know in teaching. We have chosen the topics we think most benefit the teacher. Each letter summarises the initiative or issue and then offers a useful web link to research your interest in it further.

A is for Assessment for Learning

Dealing with assessment and levels is still one of those areas that causes confusion amongst teachers. When embedded, Assessment for Learning can help to achieve dramatic results. The authority on AfL is the Assessment Reform Group at Kings College, London:

http://www.assessment-reform-group.org

B is for Boys

The underachievement of boys is still a national concern with a differential of around 10 per cent between the success of boys and girls at GCSE. The Department for Education has produced a very detailed overview of all the research around this, including strategies:

http://nationalstrategies.standards.dcsf.gov.uk/node/97208

C is for Climate for Learning

Getting the classroom climate right is a complex process involving managing behaviour, learning, interest and motivation. There are useful links that add to the ideas offered in this book:

http://www.teachingexpertise.com/articles/shaping-the-climate-for-learning-2037

D is for Discipline

Maintaining classroom discipline is the highest priority for teachers when asked in questionnaires issued by their unions. A very detailed and comprehensive report was produced by Sir Alan Steer in 2009 called *Learning Behaviour: Lessons Learned*. The definitive research paper!

http://publications.dcsf.gov.uk/eOrderingDownload/Learning-behaviour.pdf

E is for Exams

Pupils in the UK face a mass of examinations in their school life, so it is no surprise to learn that our pupils are the most assessed in the world. All the exam boards have detailed online material about their exams – from examiner feedback to past papers. The Office of Qualifications and Examinations Regulation (Ofqual) is the body that regulates all of them:

http://www.ofqual.gov.uk

F is for Film Clips

The phenomenal growth of YouTube, in particular, has allowed for an unprecedented opportunity to enhance the delivery of classroom content with film clips. It is a relatively simple process to find a clip and either save it or play it through an IWB or projector. A treasure trove! This link shows you how:

http://www.youtube.com/watch?v=tLrv0i1Vyj8

G is for Gifted Pupils

Schools are expected to know who their Gifted and Talented pupils are and show that they are providing an appropriate challenge for them so they can thrive and reach their potential as much as the rest of their peers. For policies and practice see:

http://nationalstrategies.standards.dcsf.gov.uk/giftedandtalented

H is for Homework

If every pupil did thirty minutes of homework for five days a week for five years of secondary school (500 hours) that would equate to an extra year of schooling (each school week is approximately 25 hours of lesson time multiplied by 40 school weeks!). A strong case for homework? Maybe! Case studies and best practice can be found here:

http://www.standards.dfes.gov.uk/homework/

I is for ICT

Information and communication technology has the potential to revolutionise learning. The ability to digitalise information has transformed our ability to locate any source of knowledge we like and then store masses of information electronically. It could even replace the teacher as knowledge giver:

http://www.ltscotland.org.uk/ictineducation/classroomresources/index.asp

J is for Jobs Abroad

Deciding to teach abroad can be the most rewarding experience. Internationally there are thousands of schools offering the English National Curriculum. Care is needed in choosing your institution as the quality of schools can range enormously. More information can be found at:

http://www.ticrecruitment.com

K is for Knowledge

The acquisition of knowledge used to be one of the primary purposes of the teacher. The information revolution of the late twentieth century now means that anyone can find the answer to virtually anything if they have access to the internet. To ensure your pupils can 'research, not search' the internet properly, see:

http://homeworktips.about.com/od/researchandreference/a/internet.htm

L is for Literacy

If pupils have poor literacy skills this can be a massive disadvantage when trying to get them to succeed in school. Everyone knows this and much has been done to try to sort out this problem. Lots can be found here:

http://nationalstrategies.standards.dcsf.gov.uk/node/97968

M is for Marking

Marking is possibly the most challenging aspect of the teacher's role. Part 2 of this book details many strategies to do this not only more effectively but also in a more manageable way. Other useful ideas can be found here:

http://bctf.ca/publications/NewsmagArticle.aspx?id=8920

N is for Numeracy

Numeracy is another one of the cross-curricular issues that schools are asked to tackle. For ideas and advice on how to improve pupils' ability to work with numbers visit:

http://nationalstrategies.standards.dcsf.gov.uk/files/downloads/pdf/95d4975b34e46 4f9221ed4fecad4f2b6.pdf

O is for Ofsted

The organisation that every teacher knows about: the Office for Standards in Education, Children's Services and Skills! To find reports on any school but also for useful publications such as which schools are 'outstanding' visit their web site. The Welsh equivalent is Estyn.

http://www.ofsted.gov.uk
http://www.estyn.gov.uk/home.asp

P is for Playground

Teachers often talk about the 'hidden curriculum' – in other words what pupils learn in school outside of the teacher's control. The playground is one place where this takes place for good and bad! This is a useful article on the culture of the school yard:

http://exposure.org.uk/pdfs/Exposure-Issue_94.pdf

Q is for QCDA

For specific information about your subject and issues that affect it you should go to the Qualifications and Curriculum Development Agency web site. All the latest initiatives and ideas on how to implement them can be found here. If you are missing any important documentation you can also download it from the site:

http://www.qcda.gov.uk

R is for Rewards

All schools have a rewards policy, usually in combination with a sanctions policy. For a best practice overview visit:

http://www.yjb.gov.uk/publications/scripts/prodView.asp?idproduct=57&eP=

S is for Standards

The best one-stop online resource for anything to do with issues in the classroom and government policies as well as best practice can be found at the standards site. Use the search facility to find what you need:

http://www.education.gov.uk/schools/teachingandlearning

T is for TES

The *Times Educational Supplement* is still the main publication for teachers wanting to keep up to date with the profession, although other papers have an educational focus too, such as *The Guardian*. Join the subject forums on the *TES* web site for a helpful insight into what is bothering other teachers as well as access to resources:

http://www.tes.co.uk
http://www.guardian.co.uk/education

U is for Underachievement

Every school is challenged to address any areas of underachievement with groups of pupils. These groups could be class-based, gender-based, year group-based or subject-based. For a comprehensive overview visit:

http://www.teachingexpertise.com/articles/tackling-school-underachievement-4089

V is for VLE

The virtual learning environment, or learning platform, is fast becoming a reality in many schools. There are a whole range of possible VLEs schools can use – from free ones, such as Moodle or Sharepoint, to commercial ones such as Kaleidos or Blackboard. The government's views on VLEs can be found here:

http://www.ofsted.gov.uk/Ofsted-home/Publications-and-research/Browse-all-by/Documents-by-type/Thematic-reports/Virtual-learning-environments-an-evaluation-of-their-development-in-a-sample-of-educational-settings

W is for Workload

There have been attempts to address the issue of workload through initiatives such as work–life balance and the establishment of Planning, Preparation and Assessment (PPA) time. Collecting money for trips and chasing slips for absent pupils is no longer the role of the teacher but is carried out elsewhere in school. *The Guardian* has a good article summarising what support you should expect:

http://www.guardian.co.uk/education/2008/aug/19/teaching.teachersworkload

X is for X (Extra)-Curricular Activities

Trips out of school can provide that unique and memorable experience for pupils, allowing the curriculum to really come alive. Remember that every school has a designated educational visits coordinator who can give you all the guidance you need. Best practice ideas can be found here:

http://www.teachingexpertise.com/e-bulletins/being-an-effective-educational-visits-coordinator-8007

Y is for Yellis

Yellis was once the main dataset used by schools to help inform teachers of the likely progress pupils should make. This has been replaced in England and Wales by a new dataset from the Fischer Family Trust:

http://www.fischertrust.org

Z is for ZZZZZZ

'Toxic sleep' is a term used to describe the lack of quality sleep many adolescents experience. This naturally affects their studies and can have detrimental effects on school performance. This article provides an overview of the issue:

http://www.timesonline.co.uk/tol/life_and_style/health/child_health/article6916053.ece

All web sites were live when this book went to press. If you experience difficulties accessing any of these websites please contact Crown House Publishing (books@crownhouse.co.uk) and we will do our best to provide an alternative source of information.

Epilogue

We believe passionately that we need classrooms where, fundamentally, the students do more and the teacher does less. This is achieved through an intelligent and carefully planned process that binds all of our key principles together, rather than one that uses certain ones at the expense of others.

We know that it takes commitment to achieve this but the long-term benefit is that students no longer sit passively being 'spoon-fed' and that teaching processes are based on getting the students to do the learning first and then the teachers teach. When this happens students begin to understand better, confidence builds and they have a superior understanding of what is needed to improve results.

Until we stop 'holding the spoon' the students will want to be fed. So why should we stop spoon-feeding them? It's simple. It does the students no good, it does employers no good and ultimately it does society no good.

Every teacher knows that the best lessons are those where the students are engaged, attentive and active. When this happens it starts to feel like a vocation rather than a job, and teachers remember why they came into teaching in the first place.

Acknowledgements

No book on teaching can ever fully credit all its sources as they are so wide ranging. The authors would like to make it clear that we have drawn our ideas from experiences both in the classroom as full time teachers and as providers of training courses. As a result we are not always sure where the ideas originated! Whilst we are unaware of any uncredited sources, if you are convinced that we have incorporated one of your ideas, please let us know.

We have worked together for nearly eight years and between us have presented courses to nearly 10,000 teachers. We would like to acknowledge the invaluable assistance of colleagues who have attended Dragonfly training courses. These teachers are responsible for taking our ideas into classrooms in schools all over the world and feeding ideas back to us on a regular basis.

To those teachers we would like to say a huge thank you. Your feedback enables us to guarantee that our ideas are based on classroom reality – and not just the latest theory.

We have sought and found inspiration from each other. Learning has indeed proven to be a two way process.

Personal thanks from the authors

Stephen Chapman, MD Dragonfly Training

I would like to say a huge thanks to my co-authors Alan and Steve, for their tremendous skill, dedication, enthusiasm and realism. I would like tell them they are fantastic teachers. Ten years ago, I had a vision of creating hands-on, practical and realistic training courses. Alan and Steve took this idea and did more than pick up the ball and run with it, they made it their own. Between them they have superbly represented Dragonfly Training in the UK and all over the world. We've worked together for nearly eight years and, between us, have presented courses to nearly 10,000 teachers. It's been a long and at times challenging journey but I can honestly say that I wouldn't have wanted it any other way. Over this period they have become more than just colleagues – I now regard them as friends. I can't think of two more inspiring teachers to work with and I've learnt so much from them both. Ultimately that's what it's all about.

I would also like to thank a few of my own teachers who particularly inspired me in days gone by. The legendary Cecil James of Coed Glas Junior school epitomises everything that a good teacher should be. He inspired thousands of students over the course of his amazing career and I was delighted to have the honour of speaking at his retirement function. Cecil's approach to teaching was underpinned by his belief in the immeasurable value of extracurricular activities and it is in this wider sense that he gave so much to the job.

I would also like to thank Arnold Evans of Llanishen High School who greatly enhanced my love of literature and always made me think. I'm not sure if he used even one of the strategies in this book but boy, did he know his subject! I've never forgotten the comment he wrote in one of my English essays. My sentence read: '… and so the Dr Jekyll replaces the Mr Hyde in Macbeth's character'. Next to this he wrote in the margin: 'You have compared one of the greatest plays in the English language to a cheap Victorian thriller – you stupid boy.' His methods were definitely 'old school' – and all the better for it.

I would also like to thank the family of the late and great Dr Martin Booth, who ran the PGCE History course at Cambridge where I was a student from 1989–1990. He was a totally inspirational figure to so many of us, and I hope he knew it.

I'd also like to extend a massive thank you to my wife Mary (who still works at the chalkface). She has been of immense help to me throughout the writing of this book. She helped with so many things that it's impossible to know where to start but suffice to say that without her this book would not have been written.

I'd also like to thank her sister the author Susan Elderkin for her proofreading skills.

I had better mention my children Sophie and Toby who spurred me on with such constructive comments as, 'Why do you want to write a book on teaching, Daddy? Why can't you write about something fun?' Thanks, kids!

My dear old Dad must also be mentioned in dispatches not only for his invaluable feedback but for all those times he froze his bottom off watching me play sport as a child. He continues to give the correct amount of constructive criticism and fatherly love that make him the master of what I know is a difficult job.

Lastly, I'd like to dedicate this book to my late mother, Lena Chapman, who gave me all the love, confidence and support I needed in order to spread my wings and fly. She was the best Mum you could ever have.

Steve Garnett

Firstly and probably breaking with convention, I would like to thank my wife Nicola and our four wonderful children. Though this kind of work sometimes necessitates long spells working away, their love and understanding is always there and I am always happiest when on my way home.

When co-authoring a book like this there are of course many other people to thank and acknowledge. Principally I want to thank Steve Chapman. For someone like me looking to try and make some small difference to youngsters in classrooms, Steve gave me the opportunity to spread my wings and I have never looked back. Over the last seven years I have had the privilege of training over 5,000 teachers in the ideas suggested in this book. This has taken me on a wonderful journey both metaphorically and literally, not only around the UK but latterly into Europe, the Middle East and the Far East too. For this Steve, a big thanks!

My 'partner in crime' for a lot of this work has been Alan Jervis. Alan has always been a fantastic sounding board and has a positive energy like no one else I know. Long may our journey together continue. Cheers Alan!

Finally to all the teachers who have attended courses that I have run. Judging by their feedback, they have enjoyed listening and working with the ideas contained within this book. They continue to inspire me and I thank them.

Alan Jervis

I would like to echo Stephen Chapman's thanks to my co-authors, Big Steve and Little Steve. Steve Chapman gave me my chance to become a trainer ten years ago. From the early days of brain-based learning courses, he has always been there with sound advice. Steve Garnett joined the training company later and became a travelling companion from Bangkok to the Middle East. Together they have made a massive impact on my teacher training.

Mr Benniston, of William Rhodes Secondary school, will always be the most important figure in my schooldays. He motivated so many students to be better than they thought they could be. If you could cut him in half, he would have teacher written all the way through, like Blackpool rock.

I have worked with hundreds of teachers in six different schools and there hasn't been a finer teacher than Ron Mathieson, a science teacher at Duchess's Community High School. His enthusiasm for learning was infectious and his approach to teaching was challenging and supportive.

I would like to thank my wife, Andrea. She was a social worker to the very students that I used to teach in Alnwick. She has given me total support during my training trips with flasks of coffee and encouragement on the end of a phone when I am hotelling

I need to thank my Mum and Dad who learnt me to read and write and continue to drag me up the severe mountain slopes of the Lake District. Not forgetting my daughter, Natalia, who 'enjoyed' me as her biology teacher.

Follow-up training

We sincerely hope that you have enjoyed this book and have found the concepts promoted as useful as the teaching strategies themselves. Reading this book is a fantastic start in making positive changes to improving the classroom performance in your teaching methods but if you want to take things further then it's probably best to experience it for yourself.

Improving Classroom Performance has been delivered by the Dragonfly Training team as a training day to many schools in various formats and we have now merged these together to form one comprehensive training programme that can be delivered to your school.

Each of the three authors can deliver a training day, based upon this book, at your school in a time frame to suit you. Each author has their own slant and version of the programme but you can be sure that it will conform to the Dragonfly promise of being totally practical and delivered in a hands-on and entertaining manner.

For further information about Dragonfly Training please contact us:

Tel: +44 (0)29 2071 1787
Fax: +44 (0)29 2071 1713
Email: info@dragonfly-training.co.uk
Web site: www.dragonfly-training.co.uk

Show-me Boards® are available from www.show-meboards.co.uk

Praise for *Improving Classroom Performance*

Three heads are usually better than one, and when they belong to three expert trainers in the art of teaching, the resulting compendium is likely to be very good indeed. This book does not disappoint. Written by teachers, for teachers, it eschews theory and rigid rules for lesson planning in favour of sure-fire ways of engaging interest, fostering active involvement by students and reinforcing learning. The potential of new technologies is acknowledged, but some of the ideas are delightfully low-tech, and the insistence on a variety of approaches rings true. Whatever the subject and age group you teach, however experienced or inexperienced you are, and whatever your pupils are like, there are suggestions in this book which could invigorate your teaching.

Ideally read cover to cover, but the time-pressed teacher can also dip into the 'Tools of the Trade' section for adaptable ideas. Equally welcome are the sixteen marking strategies, all of them educationally valid, but time-saving too.

I will certainly be ordering multiple copies of this book for use in staff development, and wholly recommend it. It is a timely reminder of how teaching and learning can be both productive and fun.

Valerie White, Senior Teacher, Staff Development, The King's School, Macclesfield

How to avoid 'bruised knee syndrome', harness the latest technologies and appeal to teachers in all stages of their career – it's all here. The authors are practising teachers and can claim to have led training for over 10,000 teachers, ours included. In Part 1 they lead the reader through six key principles of effective teaching and learning. Part 2, 'At the Chalkface', alone would transform the classroom climate of any teacher in their early years in the profession.

The largest part of the book is the comprehensible 'Tools of the Trade'. Forty-five practical strategies are offered to chunk learning into twenty minutes of challenge and engagement. These applications are differentiated, demonstrate progress and would doubtless satisfy an Ofsted inspector. Other suggested approaches would stimulate interest and enthusiasm for students for longer periods of learning, such as double lessons on wet and windy afternoons.

The structure of the book is user-friendly for beginning teachers as well as more experienced professionals who want to take a fresh look at their practice. The creative and imaginative tips are accompanied by clear illustrations and practical examples from different areas of the curriculum. In addition it is an ideal resource for staff professional learning sessions.

Improving Classroom Performance: Practical Applications for Effective Teaching and Learning does what it says on the tin. All school departments should have a copy.

Hilary Keens, Assistant Head, Regents Park Community College, Southampton

I really like books that offer practical strategies and that is exactly what this book does. I also like books that you can dip in and out of, and this is also achieved. I have been fortunate to attend courses run by Stephen Chapman and Alan Jervis and I think this book captures the essence of their training – fun, engaging activities, supported with no-frills educational thinking and lots and lots of try now tasks.

I really liked the approach of 'do first, teach after' to get the learners going on something, then to unpick the thinking later. I also very much liked the idea that the learners were producing the resources for the teacher and that the activities are easy to set up. You read about it before the lesson and can have it prepared quickly. The activities work – I've already tried many of them – and the feedback from classes is positive.

As well as the practical activities, the other parts of the book are very useful. Part 2, 'At the Chalkface' is great for staff training – I've used it with NQTs and for training teachers. Part 1 on key principles is educationally sound without being overblown. It condenses current thinking into something manageable for the busy teacher. The best handbook for busy classroom practitioners since *The Teacher's Toolkit* by Paul Ginnis.

This book is fun – you can't say that about much educational material. I hope some politicians and policy makers look at it and, instead of a curriculum forced on learners because it vaguely recalls their dewy-eyed memories of a public school education, they shape a curriculum which is about engagement.

Glen Alexander, Deputy Head, Archbishop Ilsley Catholic Technology College, Birmingham

This book is full of hands-on and immediately practical ideas that can really help improve learning – suitable for a teacher straight out of college or the experienced old hand. The best thing is that you can see these ideas working in almost any classroom and for different age groups. Teachers will love it because they can use these the very next day. If I was still a head at a school I would make sure all my teachers had a copy in their classroom!

Andrew Wigford, Director, Teachers International Consultancy

With experience as teachers, observers and trainers, Stephen Chapman, Steve Garnett and Alan Jervis of Dragonfly Training have produced a timely treasure chest of a book which will inspire new teachers as well as reinvigorate more experienced ones who are looking for fresh ideas free of jargon. This is a handbook for bringing the best out of teachers and learners alike. With strategies that apply across most subjects, along with insights into educational research that directly impacts on classrooms, the prime beneficiaries from every idea on every page will be the learners.

Divided into four parts, the book looks first at six key principles of effective teaching, offering practical advice on how to keep lessons consistently successful. There is discussion of effective lesson structures, including Dragonfly's famous 'da Vinci moment'. Time-tried methods that work are reinforced, while other less effective strategies are put under the microscope. Inevitable daily difficulties are tackled honestly on a 'can do' premise: with sound principles in place the learning conversation has a much improved chance of success.

Part 2, 'At the Chalkface', takes a careful look at the details of daily classroom teaching, including the 'basics' that a new teacher is working on to become second nature (eyes, voice, body language, behaviour management, etc.), but providing a list for more experienced teachers to check back to key principles. With sections on making your teaching life easier (the teacher doing less so the learner does more), marking, rewards and using ICT to the maximum, there is good up-to-date advice on a mixture of lasting favourites and newer questions: Are there different ways of marking? Am I praising students in the best possible way? How else could I arrange the classroom? Is my room a 'classroom for learning'?

'Tools of the Trade' presents forty-five teaching ideas to improve learning dramatically. Clear descriptions, helpful illustrations and a summary enhance a new toolkit for today's teachers. The essential spirit of conversation between teacher and learner is retained, but learners are actively involved and drawn into creative ideas. There are suggestions here for every teacher to pick from: the 'tools' will easily suit different teaching styles.

The final part, 'The A to Z of Teaching', contains twenty-six topics to help teachers. Brief discussions are followed by useful web links for further research. From Assessment for Learning to ZZZZZZ (toxic sleep), from Virtual Learning Environments to Discipline, the topics and links are many and varied and will sit comfortably for reference alongside any teacher's computer.

This is a very welcome addition to modern books on teaching techniques. An Aladdin's Cave of practical ideas that work, it will be of interest to anyone who is dedicated to successful classrooms where learners are inspired to learn more and teachers are supported to reflect on and develop their skills. Open Sesame!

Andrew Brown, Director of Professional Development, Marlborough College, Wiltshire

Forget the spoon-feeding and bring back the creativity into teaching and learning. This is the message that runs through this excellent book for teachers, alongside practical ideas that will strike a welcome chord with new and experienced teachers alike.

In an easy-to-read layout, the authors explain the key principles that underpin successful and stimulating teaching, such as the benefits of a starter and plenary to catch pupils' interest when their attention span is at its peak. 'At the Chalkface' offers clear and simple ways to improve your teaching, including how to make your teaching voice really work for you in the classroom, using IWBs and VLEs to good effect and how to make your classroom the place every student wants to be in. The forty-five 'Tools of the Trade' are what every teacher needs to know – ideas that will bring the joy back into teaching and allow teachers to inspire and stimulate their students.

The authors bring their collective wealth of classroom experience to this excellent collection of practical and sure-fire strategies for improving the teaching and learning experience. If you have only one teaching manual on your desk, this is the one.

Victoria Pugh, Deputy Head, Taunton Preparatory School

I really enjoyed reading this and am pleased to see it in type – having been on several Dragonfly courses my notes have never done justice to all the ideas. This book either reminds me of some I'd forgotten or clarifies how to do them. I've used several activities for a couple of years now, especially 'Seven Monkeys' to great effect.

Jill Owen, 'Newly Invigorated' Science Teacher, Bryngwyn School, Llanelli